SPIDER-MAN
MILES MORALES

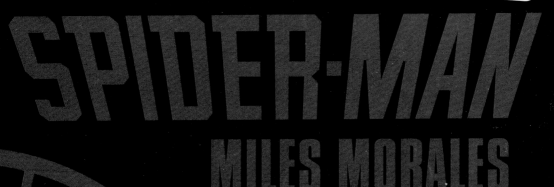

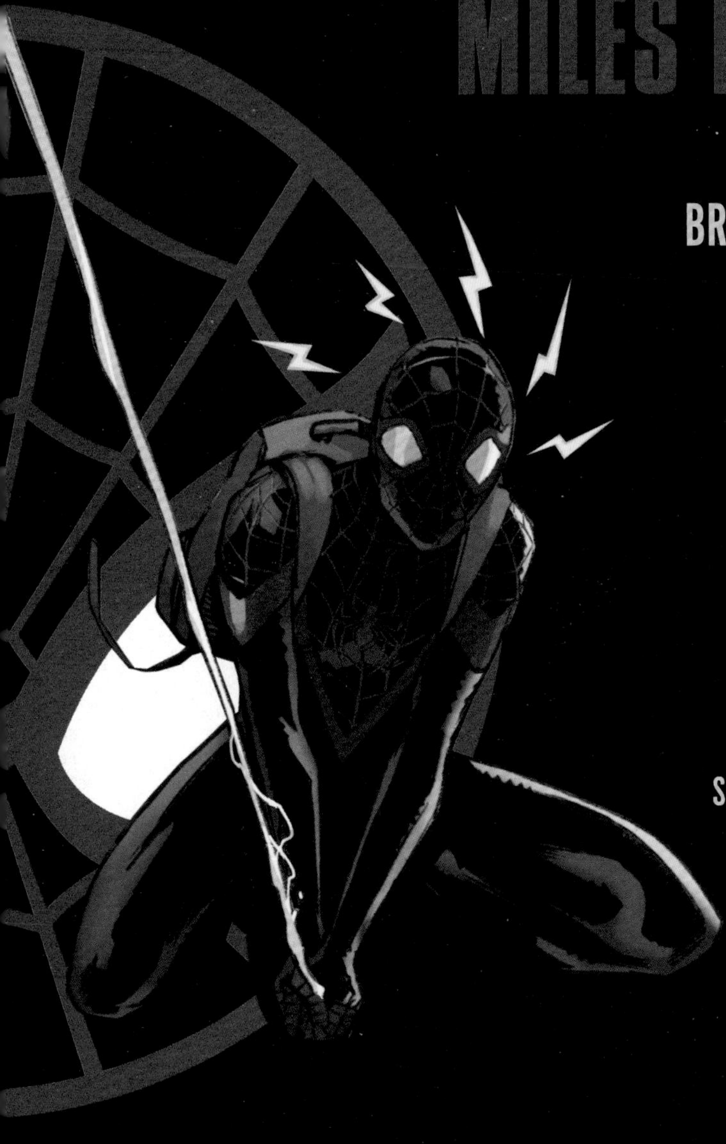

BRIAN MICHAEL BENDIS
writer

SARA PICHELLI
artist

GAETANO CARLUCCI
inking assist

JUSTIN PONSOR
colorist

VC'S CORY PETIT
letterer

SARA PICHELLI & JUSTIN PONSOR
cover art

DEVIN LEWIS
assistant editor

NICK LOWE
editor

collection editor JENNIFER GRÜNWALD
associate editor SARAH BRUNSTAD
editor, special projects MARK D. BEAZLEY
vp, production & special projects JEFF YOUNGQUIST
svp print, sales & marketing DAVID GABRIEL
book designer ADAM DEL RE

editor in chief AXEL ALONSO
chief creative officer JOE QUESADA
publisher DAN BUCKLEY
executive producer ALAN FINE

SPIDER-MAN created by
STAN LEE & STEVE DITKO

SPIDER-MAN: MILES MORALES VOL. 1. Contains material originally published in magazine form as SPIDER-MAN #1-5. First printing 2016. ISBN# 978-0-7851-9961-8. Published by MARVEL WORLDWIDE, INC., a subsidiary of MARVEL ENTERTAINMENT, LLC. OFFICE OF PUBLICATION: 135 West 50th Street, New York, NY 10020. Copyright © 2016 MARVEL. No similarity between any of the names, characters, persons, and/or institutions in this magazine with those of any living or dead person or institution is intended, and any such similarity which may exist is purely coincidental. Printed in Canada. ALAN FINE, President, Marvel Entertainment; DAN BUCKLEY, President, TV, Publishing & Brand Management; JOE QUESADA, Chief Creative Officer; TOM BREVOORT, SVP of Publishing; DAVID BOGART, SVP of Business Affairs & Operations, Publishing & Partnership; C.B. CEBULSKI, VP of Brand Management & Development, Asia; DAVID GABRIEL, SVP of Sales & Marketing, Publishing; JEFF YOUNGQUIST, VP of Production & Special Projects; DAN CARR, Executive Director of Publishing Technology; ALEX MORALES, Director of Publishing Operations; SUSAN CRESPI, Production Manager; STAN LEE, Chairman Emeritus. For information regarding advertising in Marvel Comics or on Marvel.com, please contact Vit DeBellis, Integrated Sales Manager, at vdebellis@marvel.com. For Marvel subscription inquiries, please call 888-511-5480. Manufactured between 7/15/2016 and 8/22/2016 by SOLISCO PRINTERS, SCOTT, QC, CANADA.

10 9 8 7 6 5 4 3 2 1

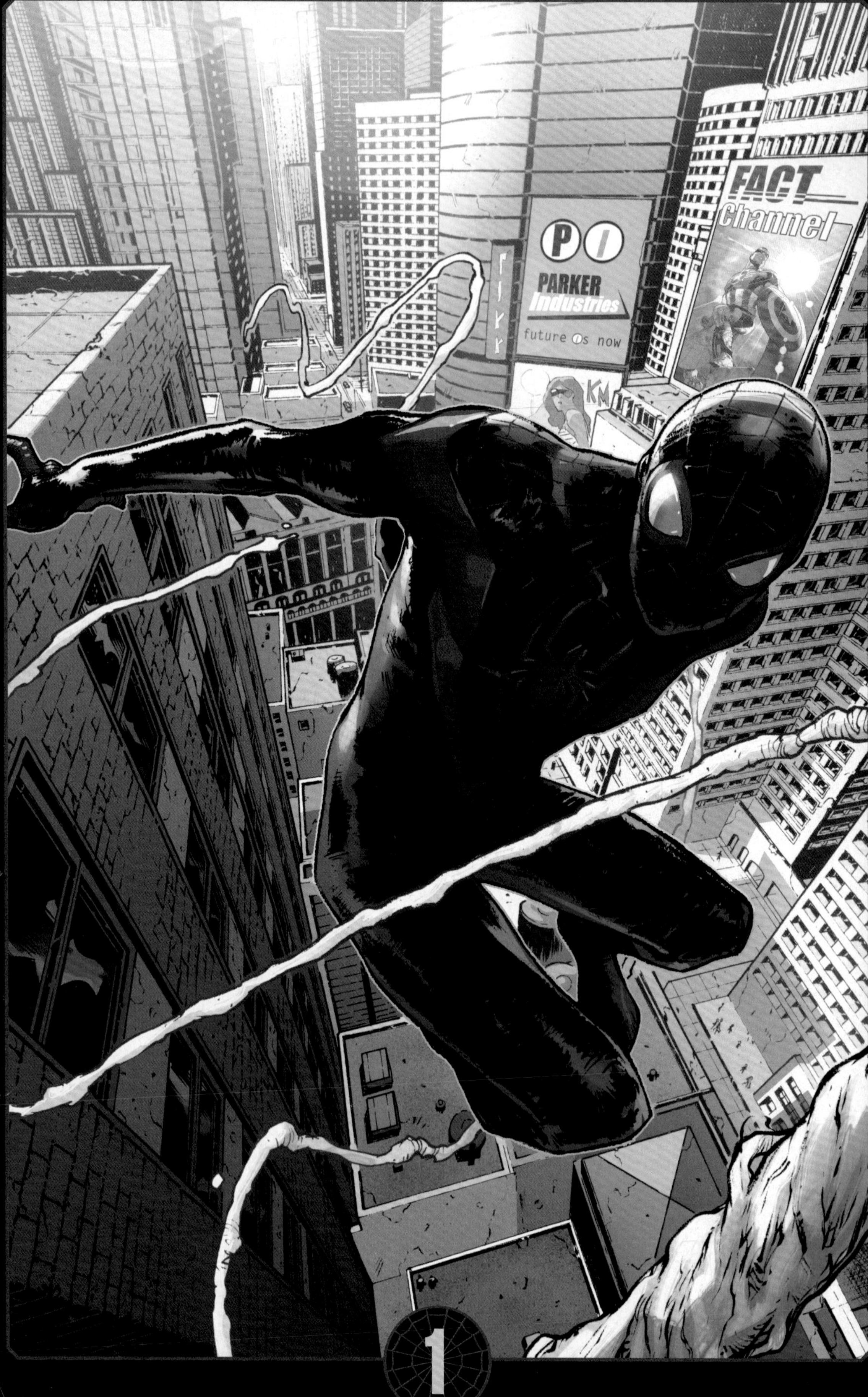
FACT
Channel
PI
PARKER
Industries
future is now
1

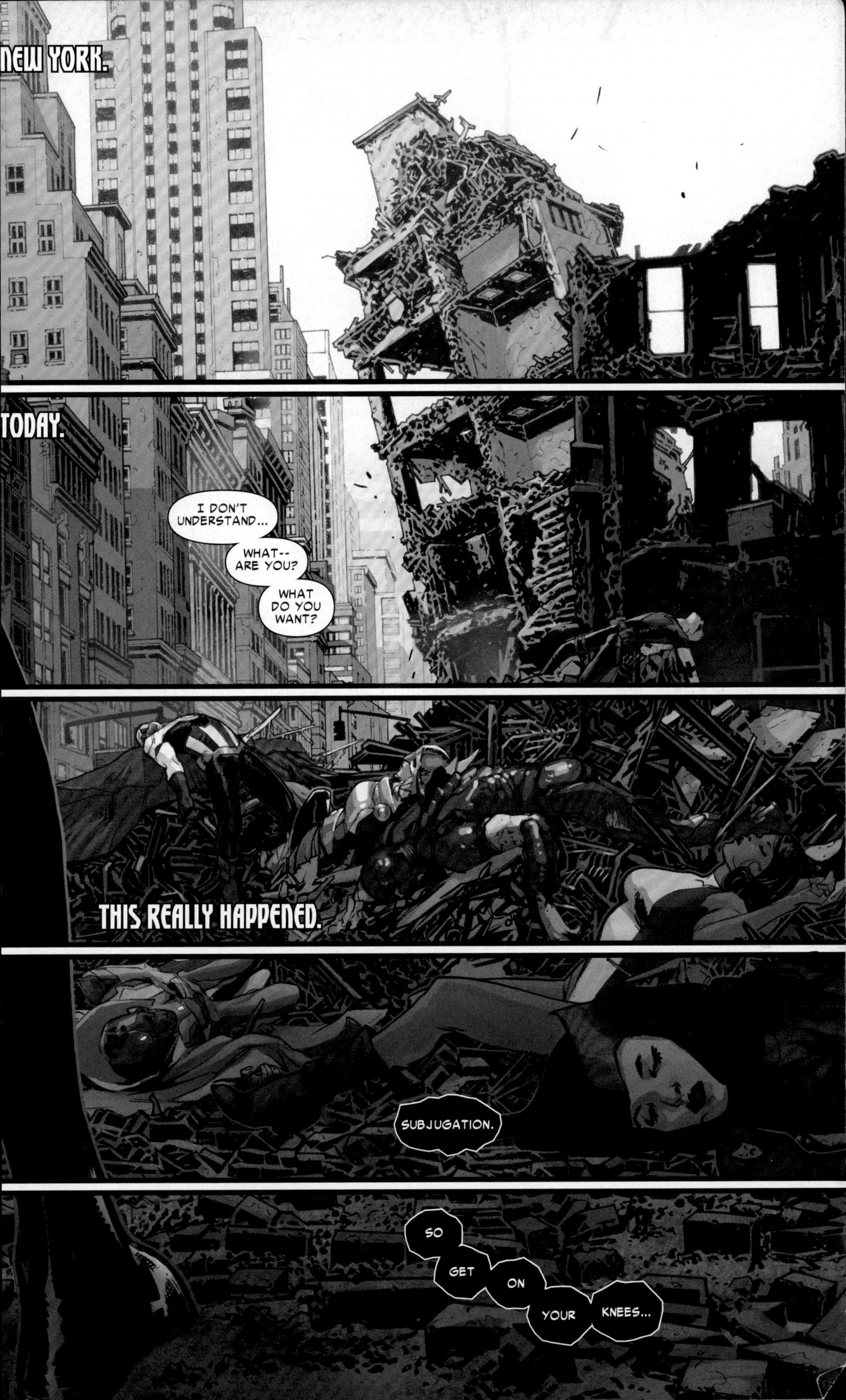
NEW YORK.
TODAY.
I DON'T UNDERSTAND...
WHAT-- ARE YOU?
WHAT DO YOU WANT?
THIS REALLY HAPPENED.
SUBJUGATION.
SO
GET
ON
YOUR
KNEES...

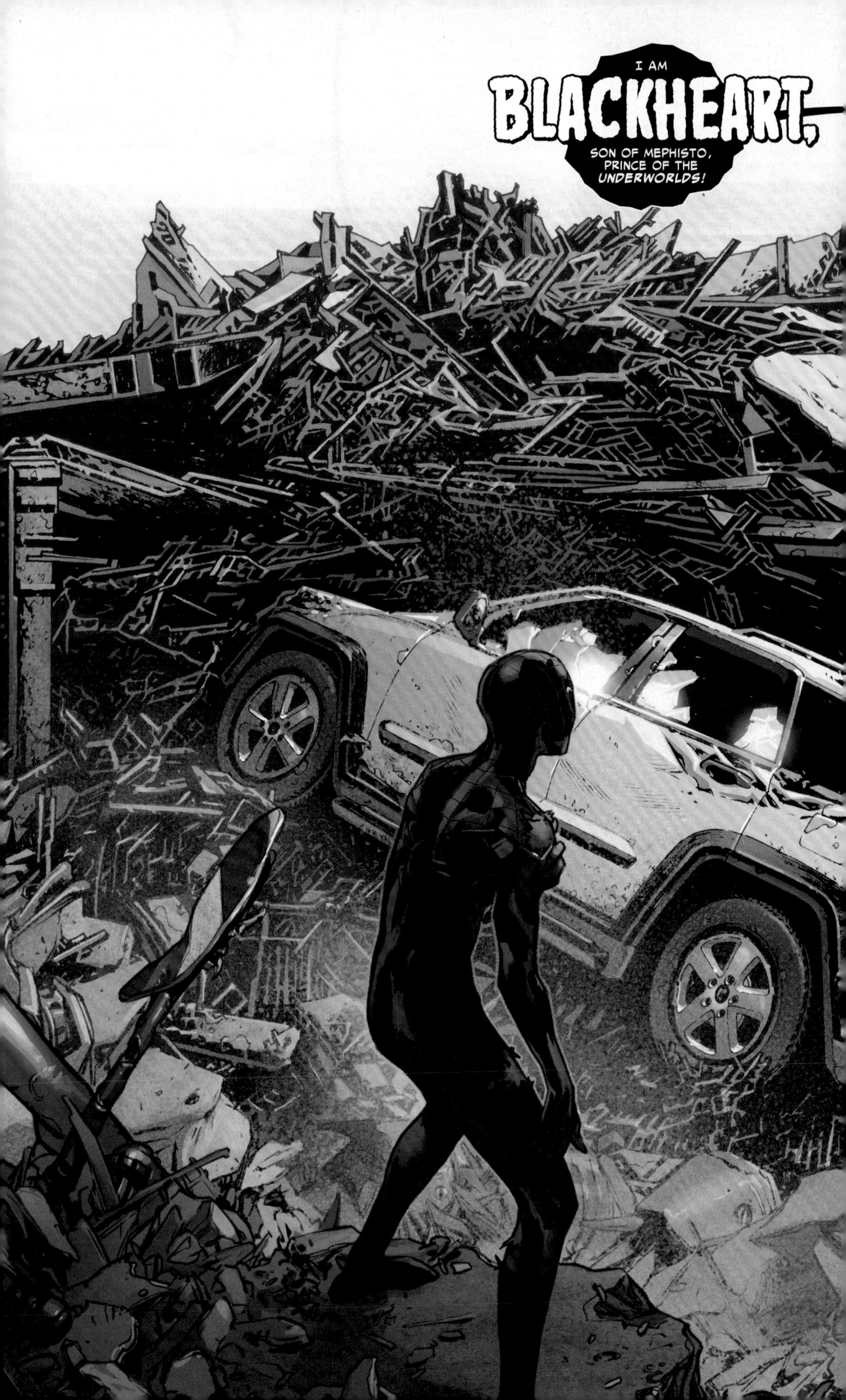
I AM
BLACKHEART,
SON OF MEPHISTO, PRINCE OF THE UNDERWORLDS!

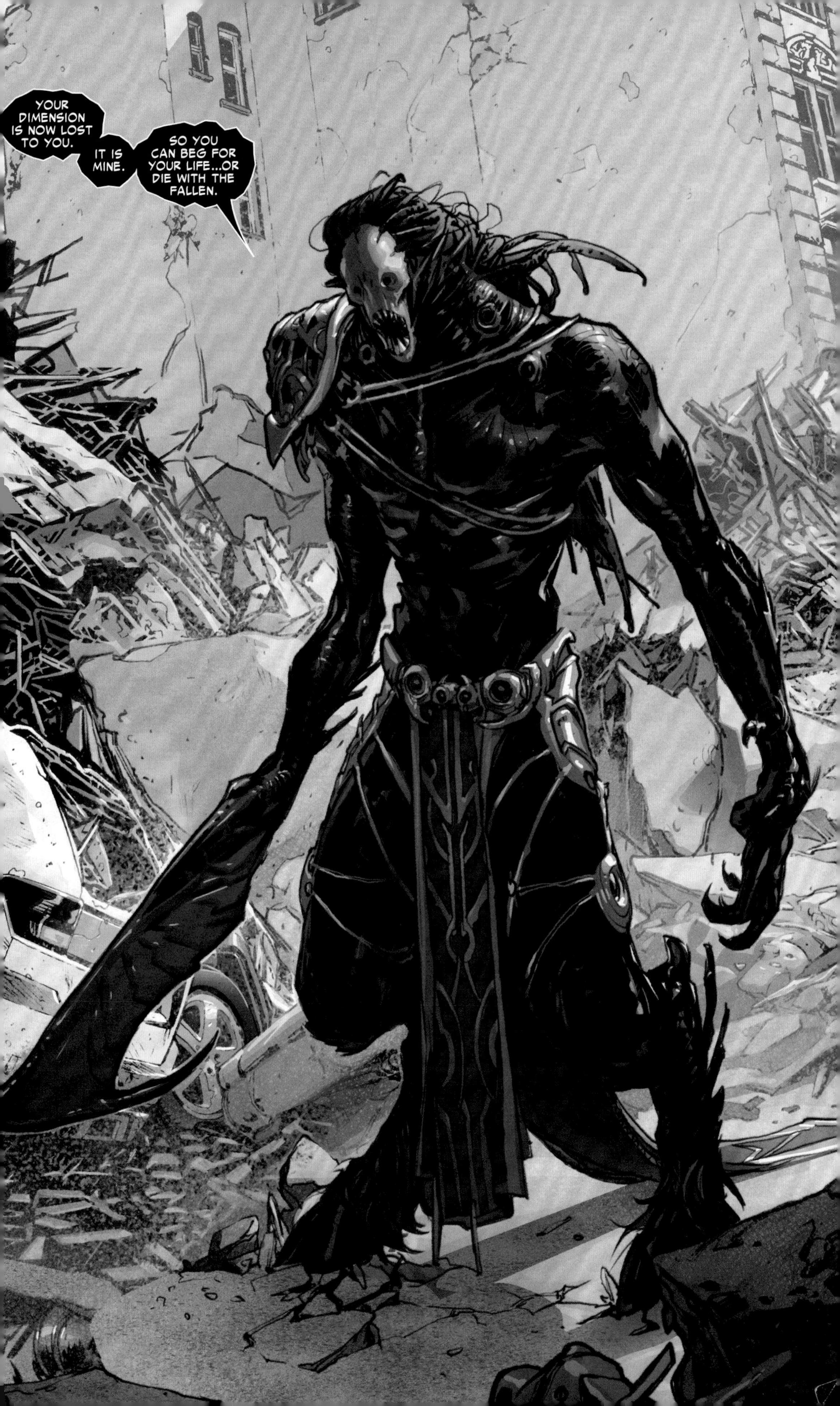
YOUR DIMENSION IS NOW LOST TO YOU.
IT IS MINE.
SO YOU CAN BEG FOR YOUR LIFE...OR DIE WITH THE FALLEN.

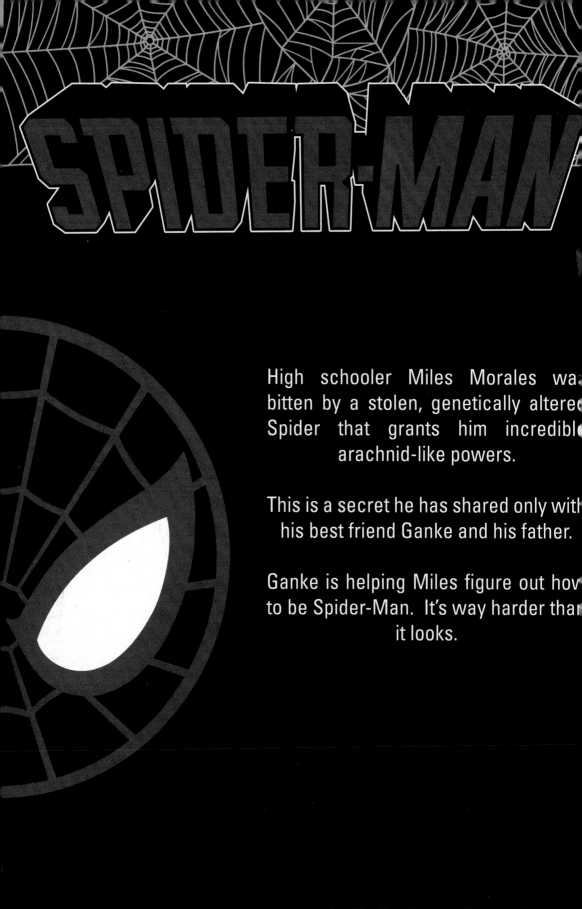

SPIDER-MAN

High schooler Miles Morales was bitten by a stolen, genetically altered Spider that grants him incredible arachnid-like powers.

This is a secret he has shared only with his best friend Ganke and his father.

Ganke is helping Miles figure out how to be Spider-Man. It's way harder than it looks.

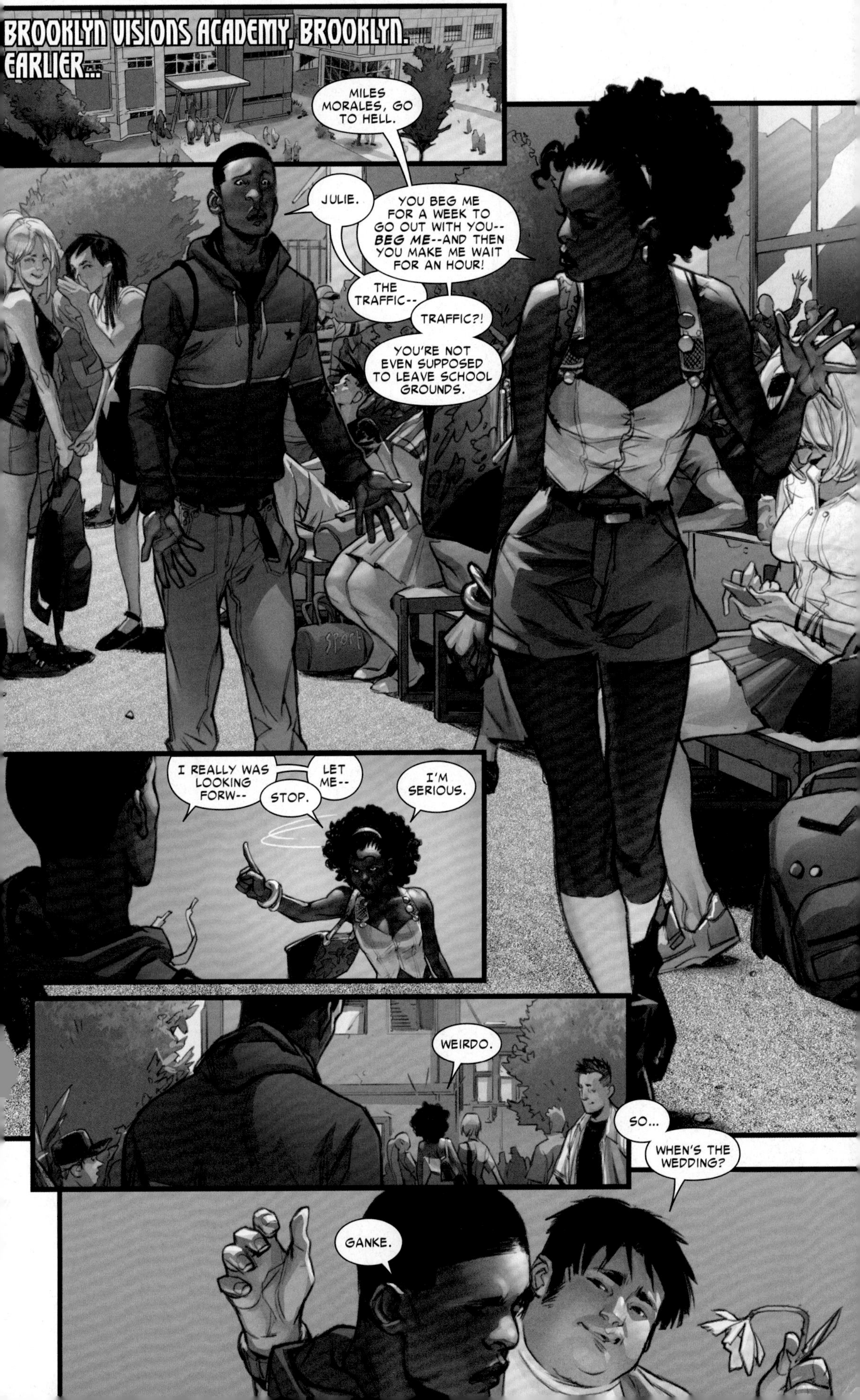
BROOKLYN VISIONS ACADEMY, BROOKLYN. EARLIER...
MILES MORALES, GO TO HELL.
JULIE.
YOU BEG ME FOR A WEEK TO GO OUT WITH YOU-- BEG ME--AND THEN YOU MAKE ME WAIT FOR AN HOUR!
THE TRAFFIC--
TRAFFIC?!
YOU'RE NOT EVEN SUPPOSED TO LEAVE SCHOOL GROUNDS.
I REALLY WAS LOOKING FORW--
STOP.
LET ME--
I'M SERIOUS.
WEIRDO.
SO...
WHEN'S THE WEDDING?
GANKE.

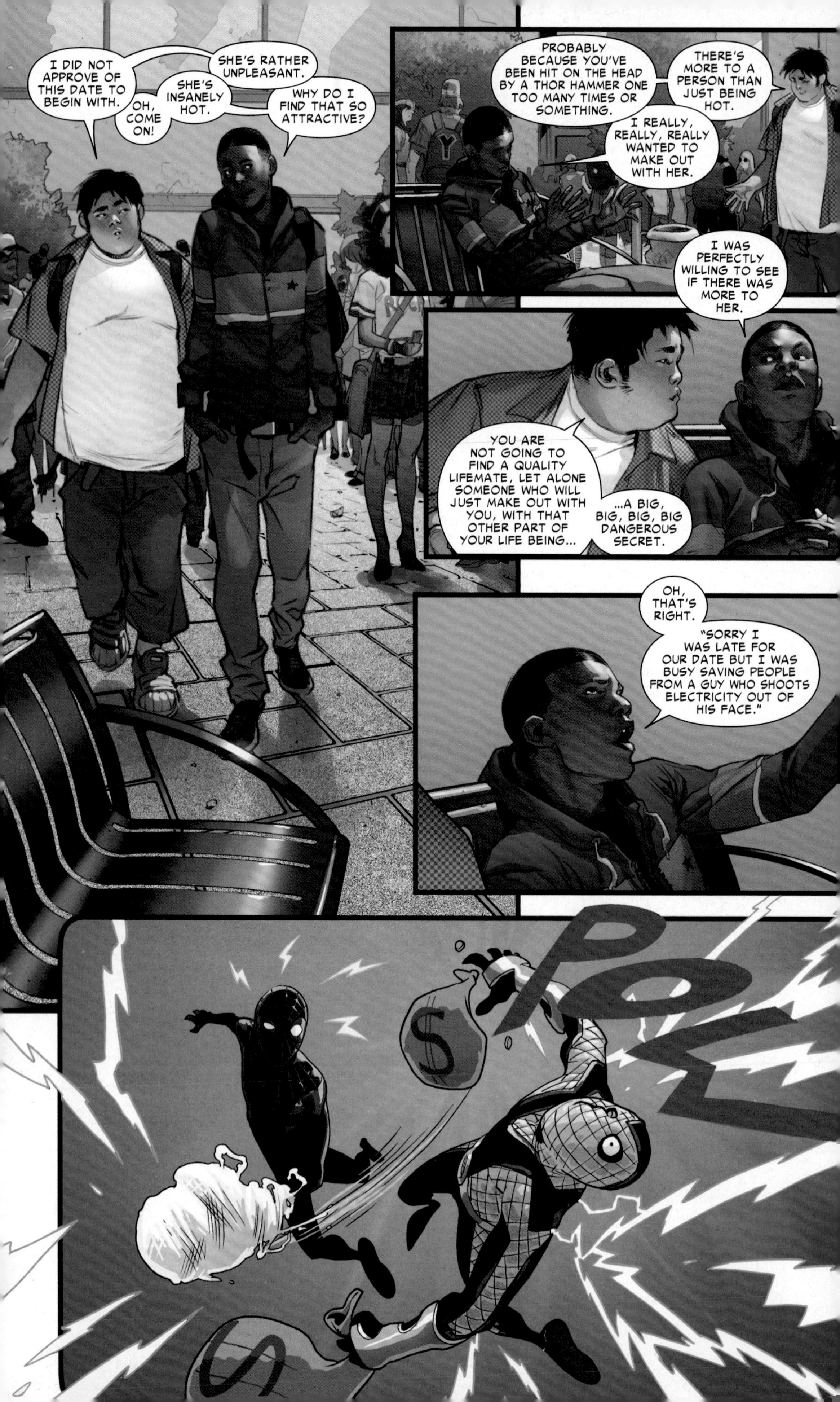
I DID NOT APPROVE OF THIS DATE TO BEGIN WITH.
SHE'S RATHER UNPLEASANT.
SHE'S INSANELY HOT.
OH, COME ON!
WHY DO I FIND THAT SO ATTRACTIVE?
PROBABLY BECAUSE YOU'VE BEEN HIT ON THE HEAD BY A THOR HAMMER ONE TOO MANY TIMES OR SOMETHING.
THERE'S MORE TO A PERSON THAN JUST BEING HOT.
I REALLY, REALLY, REALLY WANTED TO MAKE OUT WITH HER.
I WAS PERFECTLY WILLING TO SEE IF THERE WAS MORE TO HER.
YOU ARE NOT GOING TO FIND A QUALITY LIFEMATE, LET ALONE SOMEONE WHO WILL JUST MAKE OUT WITH YOU, WITH THAT OTHER PART OF YOUR LIFE BEING...
...A BIG, BIG, BIG, BIG DANGEROUS SECRET.
OH, THAT'S RIGHT.
"SORRY I WAS LATE FOR OUR DATE BUT I WAS BUSY SAVING PEOPLE FROM A GUY WHO SHOOTS ELECTRICITY OUT OF HIS FACE."
POW

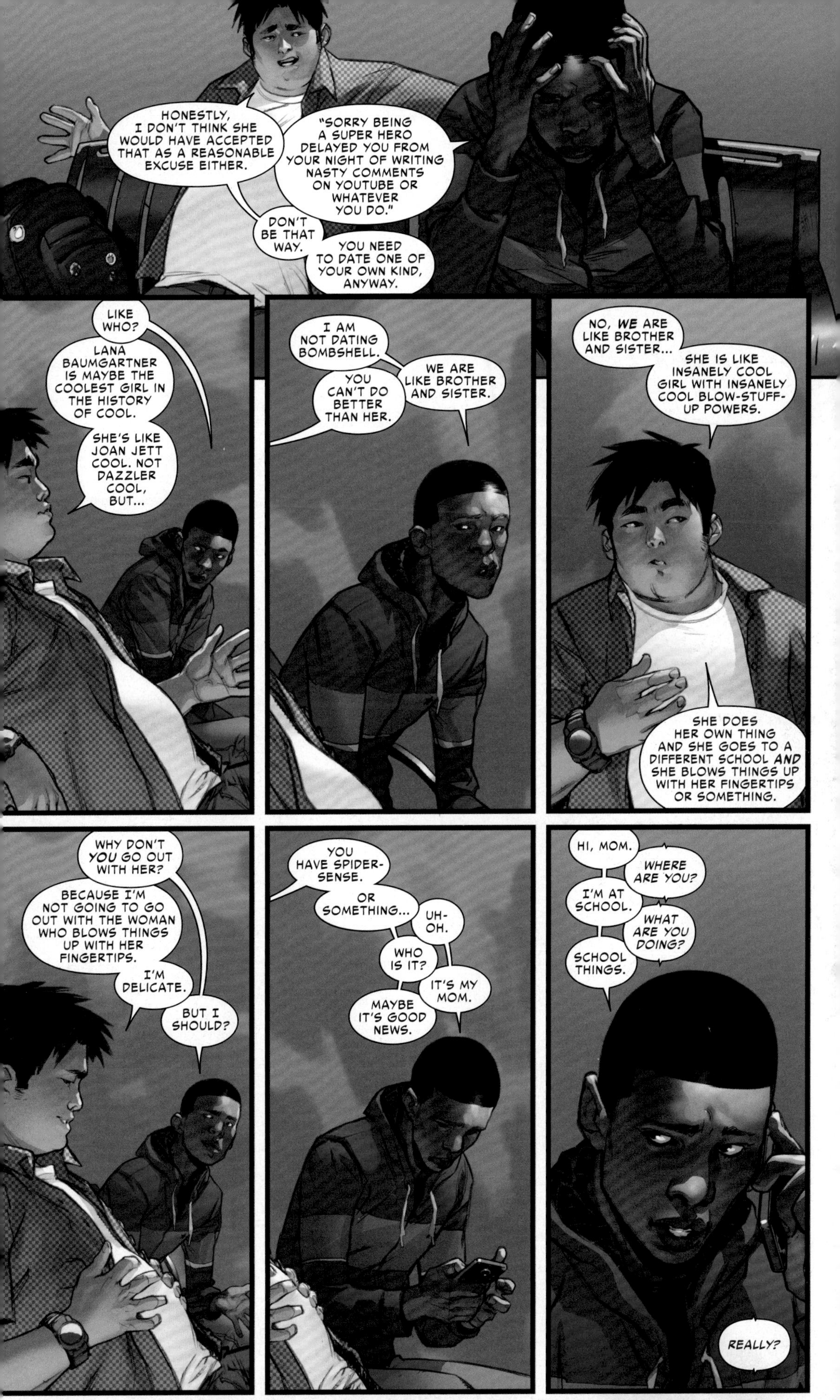

HONESTLY, I DON'T THINK SHE WOULD HAVE ACCEPTED THAT AS A REASONABLE EXCUSE EITHER.
"SORRY BEING A SUPER HERO DELAYED YOU FROM YOUR NIGHT OF WRITING NASTY COMMENTS ON YOUTUBE OR WHATEVER YOU DO."
DON'T BE THAT WAY.
YOU NEED TO DATE ONE OF YOUR OWN KIND, ANYWAY.
LIKE WHO?
LANA BAUMGARTNER IS MAYBE THE COOLEST GIRL IN THE HISTORY OF COOL.
SHE'S LIKE JOAN JETT COOL. NOT DAZZLER COOL, BUT...
I AM NOT DATING BOMBSHELL.
YOU CAN'T DO BETTER THAN HER.
WE ARE LIKE BROTHER AND SISTER.
NO, WE ARE LIKE BROTHER AND SISTER...
SHE IS LIKE INSANELY COOL GIRL WITH INSANELY COOL BLOW-STUFF-UP POWERS.
SHE DOES HER OWN THING AND SHE GOES TO A DIFFERENT SCHOOL AND SHE BLOWS THINGS UP WITH HER FINGERTIPS OR SOMETHING.
WHY DON'T YOU GO OUT WITH HER?
BECAUSE I'M NOT GOING TO GO OUT WITH THE WOMAN WHO BLOWS THINGS UP WITH HER FINGERTIPS.
I'M DELICATE.
BUT I SHOULD?
YOU HAVE SPIDER-SENSE.
OR SOMETHING...
UH-OH.
WHO IS IT?
IT'S MY MOM.
MAYBE IT'S GOOD NEWS.
HI, MOM.
WHERE ARE YOU?
I'M AT SCHOOL.
WHAT ARE YOU DOING?
SCHOOL THINGS.
REALLY?

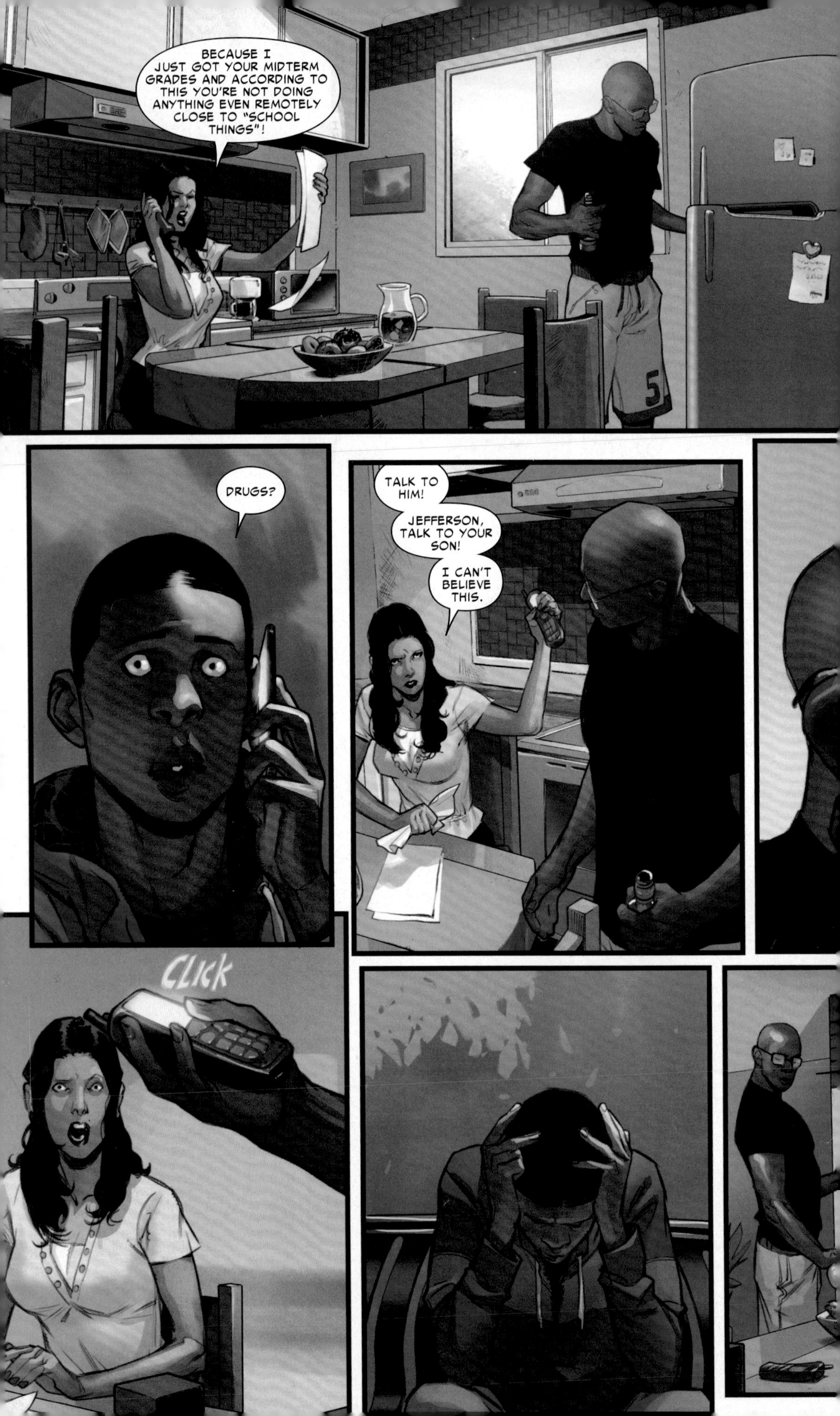
BECAUSE I JUST GOT YOUR MIDTERM GRADES AND ACCORDING TO THIS YOU'RE NOT DOING ANYTHING EVEN REMOTELY CLOSE TO "SCHOOL THINGS"!
DRUGS?
TALK TO HIM!
JEFFERSON, TALK TO YOUR SON!
I CAN'T BELIEVE THIS.
CLICK

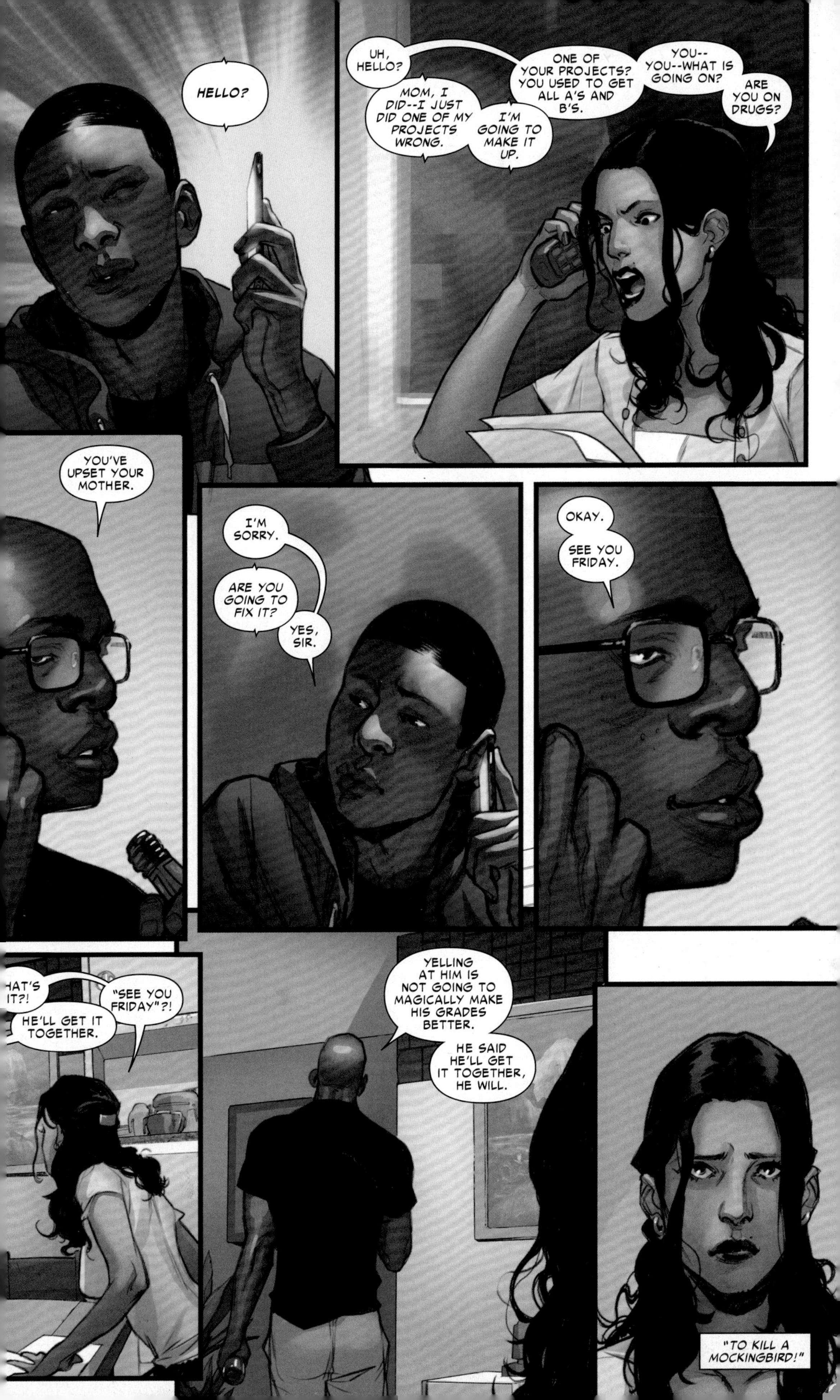
HELLO?
UH, HELLO?
MOM, I DID--I JUST DID ONE OF MY PROJECTS WRONG.
ONE OF YOUR PROJECTS? YOU USED TO GET ALL A'S AND B'S.
I'M GOING TO MAKE IT UP.
YOU-- YOU--WHAT IS GOING ON?
ARE YOU ON DRUGS?
YOU'VE UPSET YOUR MOTHER.
I'M SORRY.
ARE YOU GOING TO FIX IT?
YES, SIR.
OKAY.
SEE YOU FRIDAY.
HAT'S IT?!
"SEE YOU FRIDAY"?!
HE'LL GET IT TOGETHER.
YELLING AT HIM IS NOT GOING TO MAGICALLY MAKE HIS GRADES BETTER.
HE SAID HE'LL GET IT TOGETHER, HE WILL.
"TO KILL A MOCKINGBIRD!"

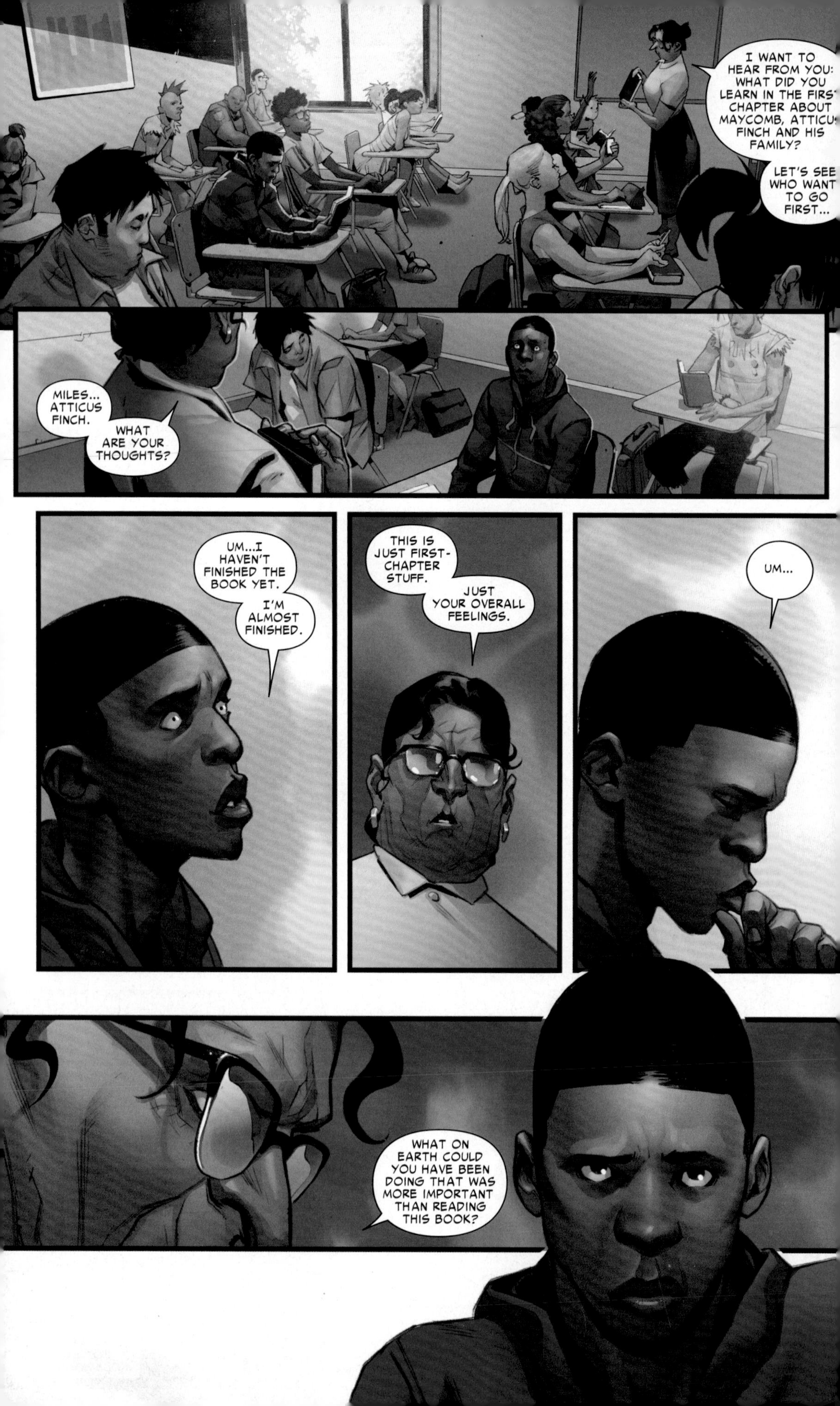

I WANT TO HEAR FROM YOU: WHAT DID YOU LEARN IN THE FIRST CHAPTER ABOUT MAYCOMB, ATTICUS FINCH AND HIS FAMILY?
LET'S SEE WHO WANT TO GO FIRST...
PUNK!
MILES... ATTICUS FINCH.
WHAT ARE YOUR THOUGHTS?
UM...I HAVEN'T FINISHED THE BOOK YET.
I'M ALMOST FINISHED.
THIS IS JUST FIRST-CHAPTER STUFF.
JUST YOUR OVERALL FEELINGS.
UM...
WHAT ON EARTH COULD YOU HAVE BEEN DOING THAT WAS MORE IMPORTANT THAN READING THIS BOOK?

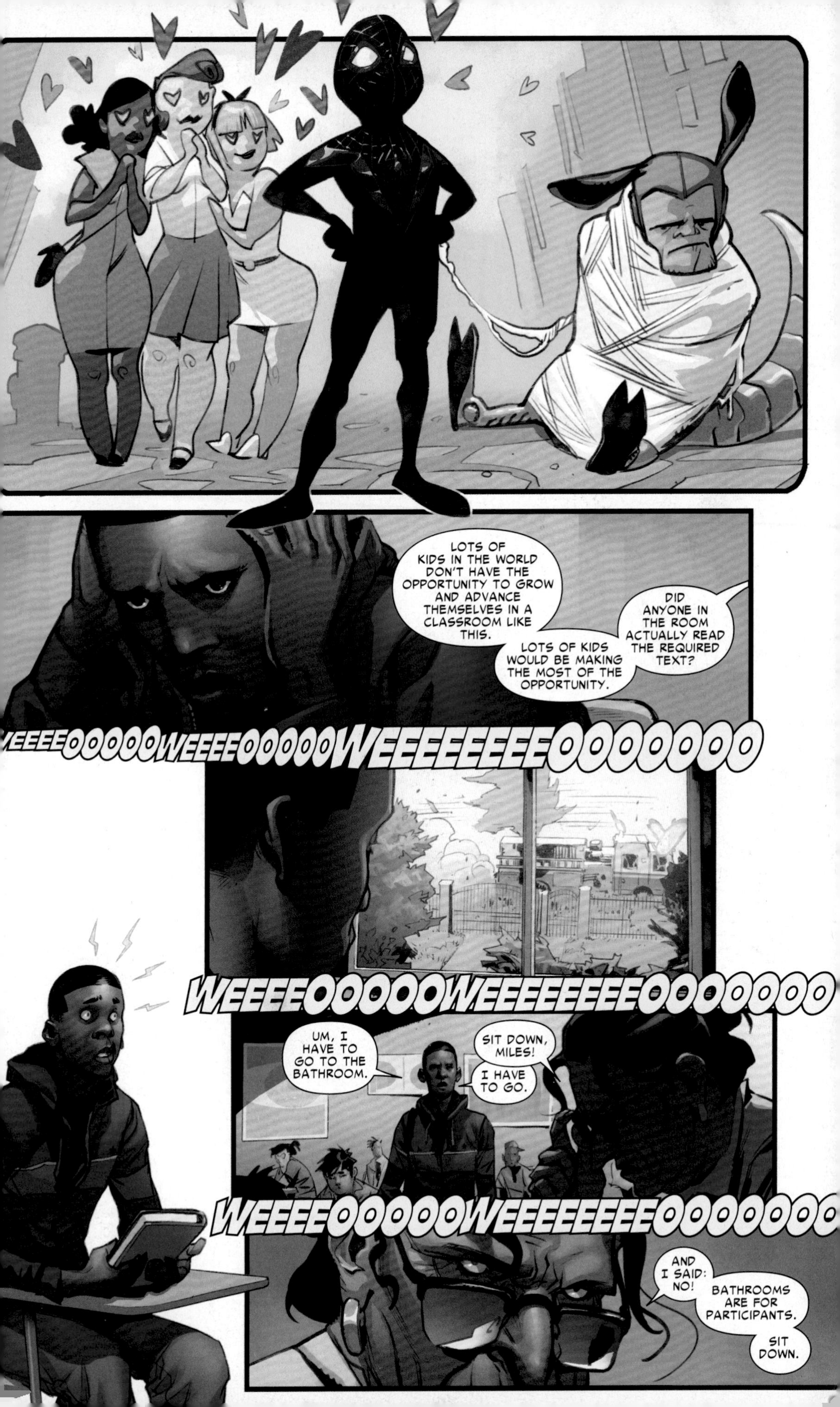

LOTS OF KIDS IN THE WORLD DON'T HAVE THE OPPORTUNITY TO GROW AND ADVANCE THEMSELVES IN A CLASSROOM LIKE THIS.
LOTS OF KIDS WOULD BE MAKING THE MOST OF THE OPPORTUNITY.
DID ANYONE IN THE ROOM ACTUALLY READ THE REQUIRED TEXT?
EEEEOOOOOWEEEEOOOOOWEEEEEEEEEOOOOOOO
WEEEEOOOOOWEEEEEEEEEOOOOOOO
UM, I HAVE TO GO TO THE BATHROOM.
SIT DOWN, MILES!
I HAVE TO GO.
WEEEEOOOOOWEEEEEEEEEOOOOOOO
AND I SAID: NO!
BATHROOMS ARE FOR PARTICIPANTS.
SIT DOWN.

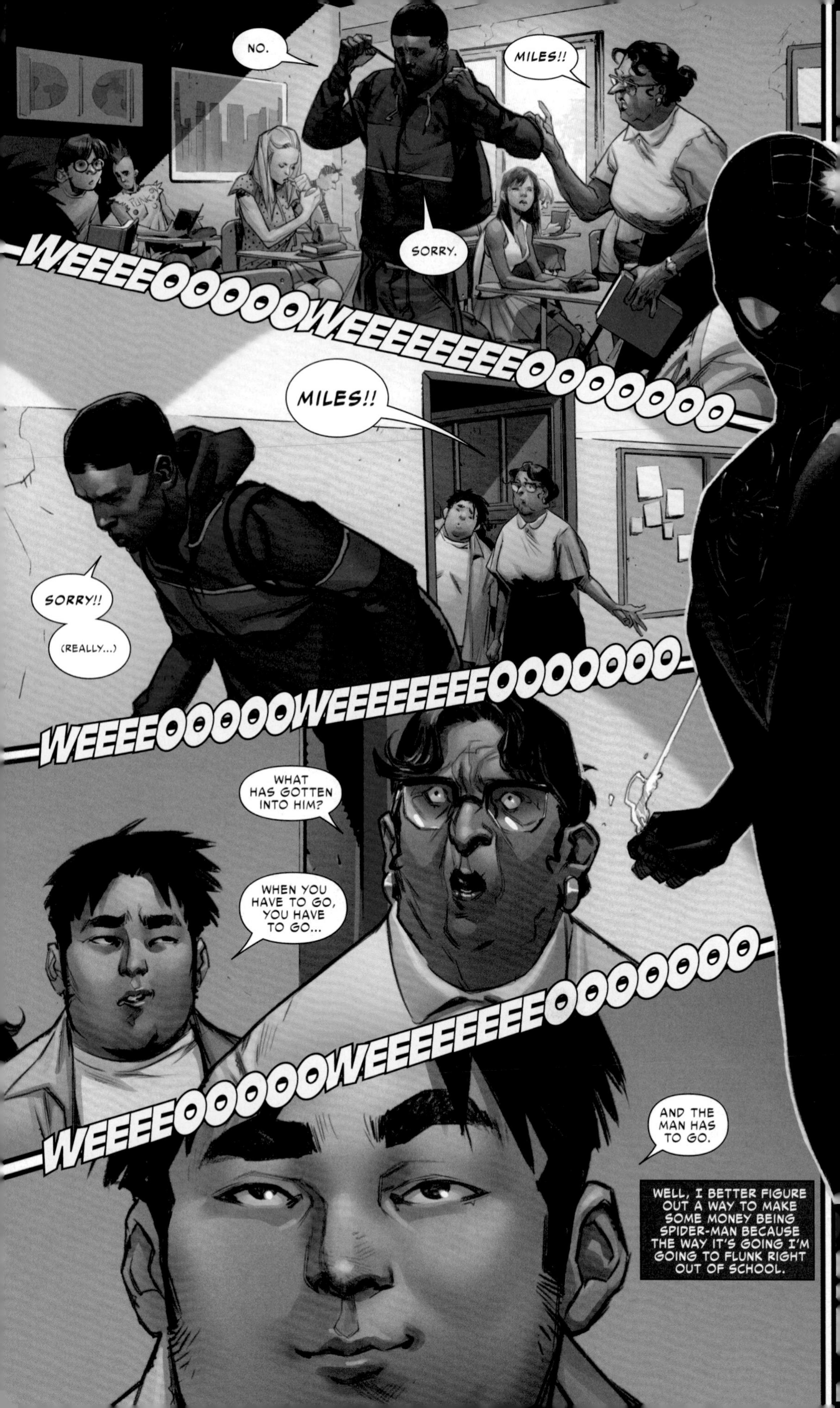

NO.
MILES!!
SORRY.
WEEEEOOOOOWEEEEEEEEEOOOOOOOO
MILES!!
SORRY!!
(REALLY...)
WEEEEOOOOOWEEEEEEEEEOOOOOOOO
WHAT HAS GOTTEN INTO HIM?
WHEN YOU HAVE TO GO, YOU HAVE TO GO...
WEEEEOOOOOWEEEEEEEEEOOOOOOOO
AND THE MAN HAS TO GO.
WELL, I BETTER FIGURE OUT A WAY TO MAKE SOME MONEY BEING SPIDER-MAN BECAUSE THE WAY IT'S GOING I'M GOING TO FLUNK RIGHT OUT OF SCHOOL.

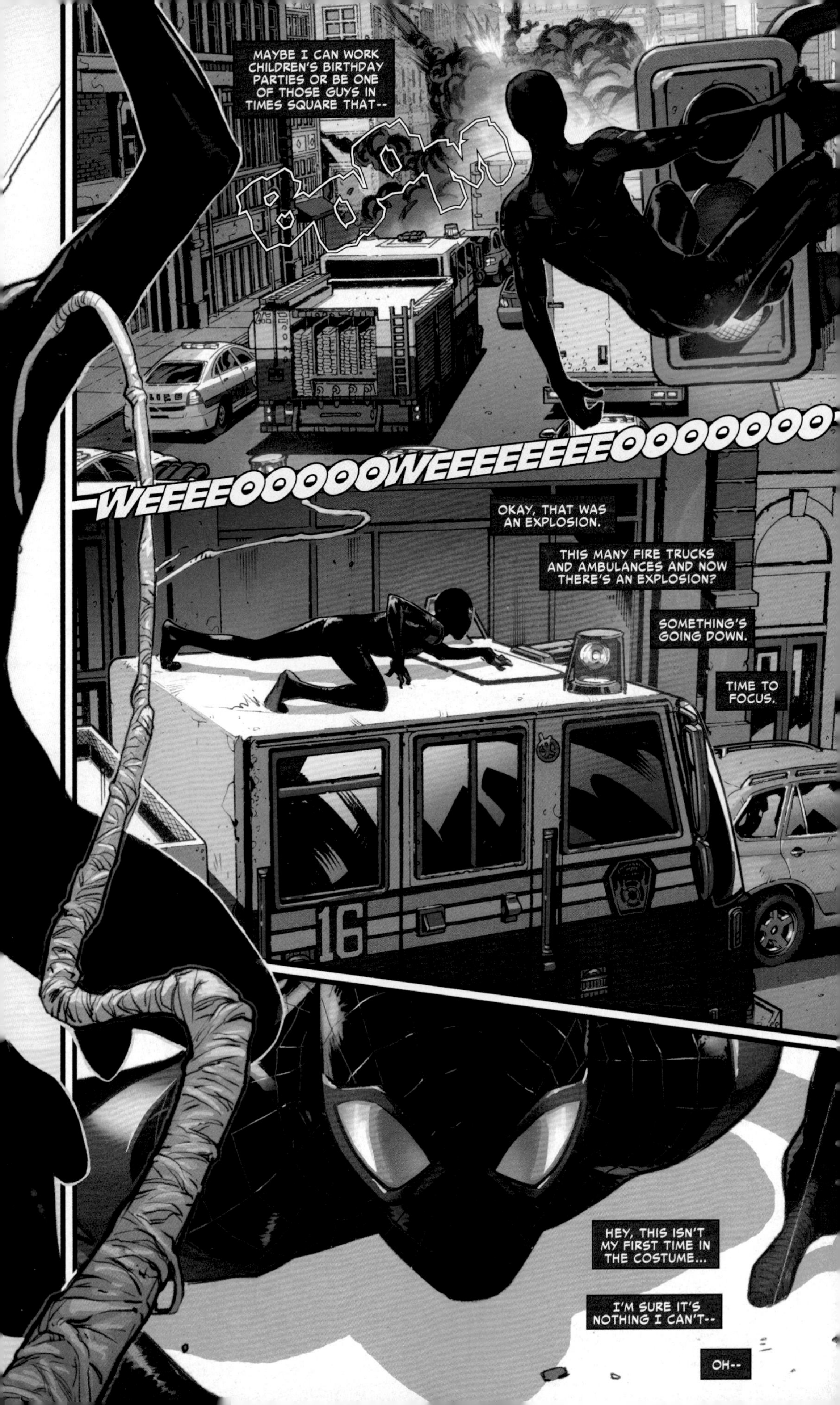

MAYBE I CAN WORK CHILDREN'S BIRTHDAY PARTIES OR BE ONE OF THOSE GUYS IN TIMES SQUARE THAT--
BOOM
WEEEEOOOOOOWEEEEEEEEOOOOOOOO
OKAY, THAT WAS AN EXPLOSION.
THIS MANY FIRE TRUCKS AND AMBULANCES AND NOW THERE'S AN EXPLOSION?
SOMETHING'S GOING DOWN.
TIME TO FOCUS.
16
HEY, THIS ISN'T MY FIRST TIME IN THE COSTUME...
I'M SURE IT'S NOTHING I CAN'T--
OH--

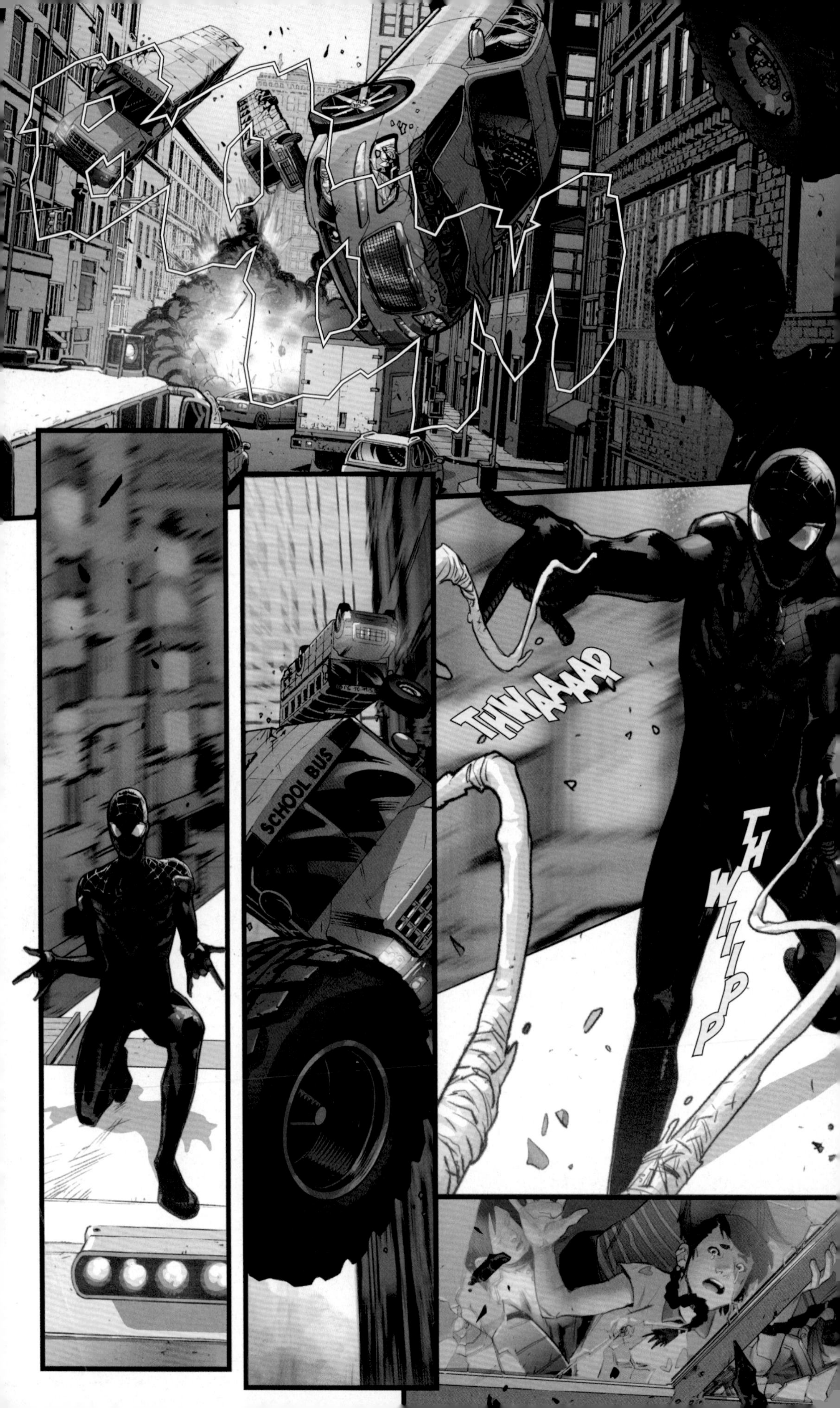
SCHOOL BUS
SCHOOL BUS
THWAAAAP
THWHIIPP

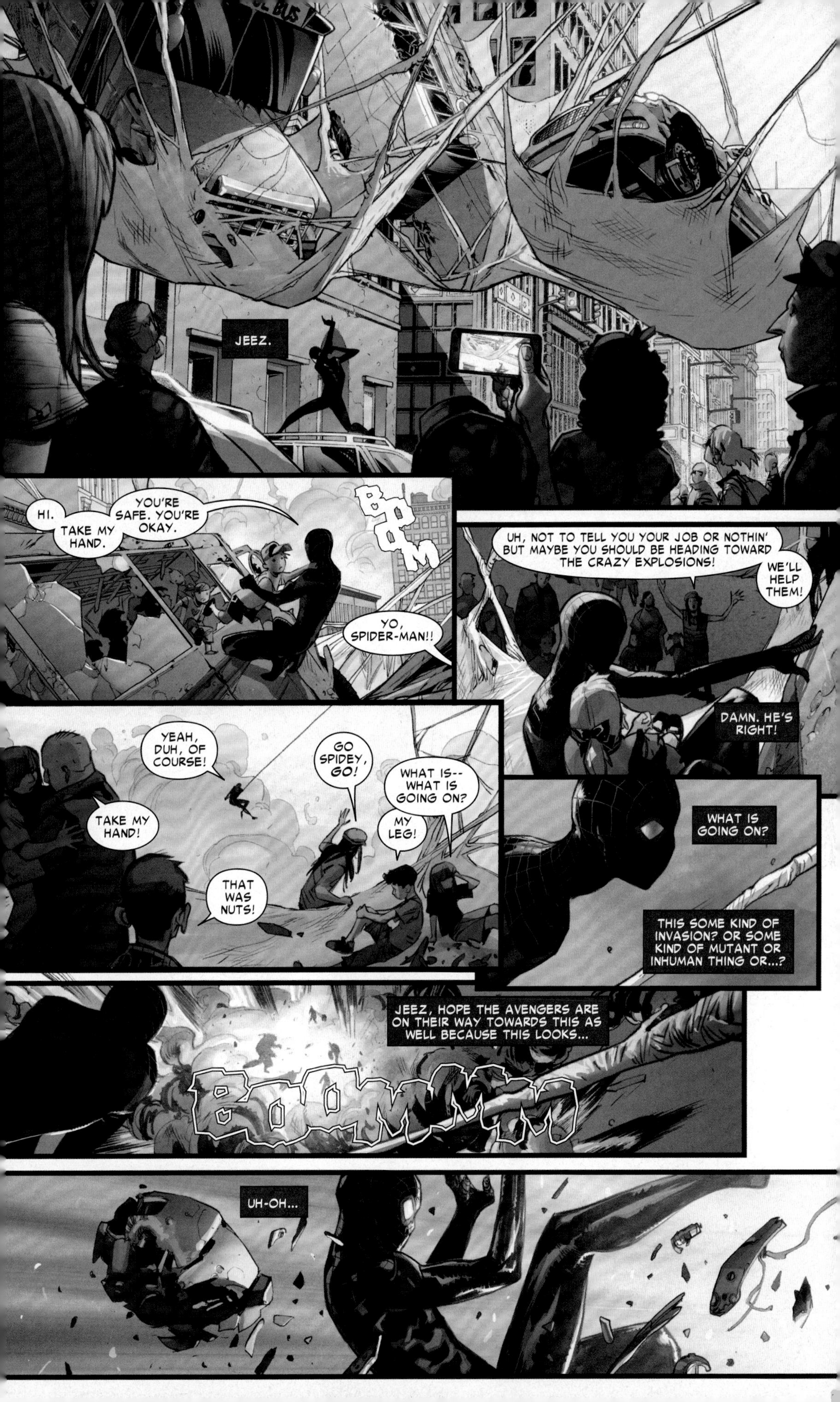

JEEZ.
HI.
TAKE MY HAND.
YOU'RE SAFE. YOU'RE OKAY.
BOOM
YO, SPIDER-MAN!!
UH, NOT TO TELL YOU YOUR JOB OR NOTHIN' BUT MAYBE YOU SHOULD BE HEADING TOWARD THE CRAZY EXPLOSIONS!
WE'LL HELP THEM!
DAMN. HE'S RIGHT!
YEAH, DUH, OF COURSE!
TAKE MY HAND!
GO SPIDEY, GO!
WHAT IS-- WHAT IS GOING ON?
MY LEG!
THAT WAS NUTS!
WHAT IS GOING ON?
THIS SOME KIND OF INVASION? OR SOME KIND OF MUTANT OR INHUMAN THING OR...?
JEEZ, HOPE THE AVENGERS ARE ON THEIR WAY TOWARDS THIS AS WELL BECAUSE THIS LOOKS...
BOOMMM
UH-OH...

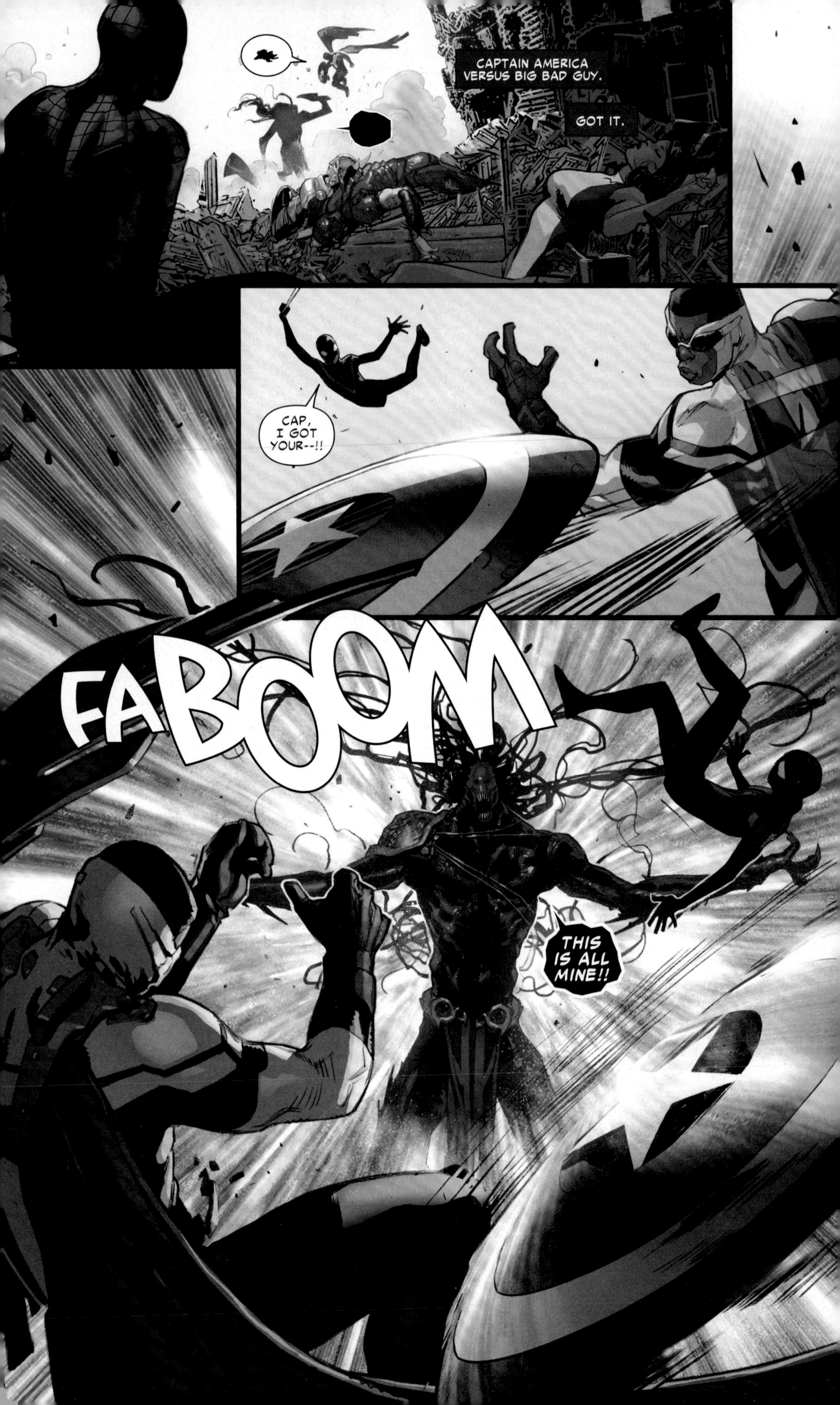
CAPTAIN AMERICA
VERSUS BIG BAD GUY.
GOT IT.
CAP,
I GOT
YOUR--!!
FABOOM
THIS
IS ALL
MINE!!

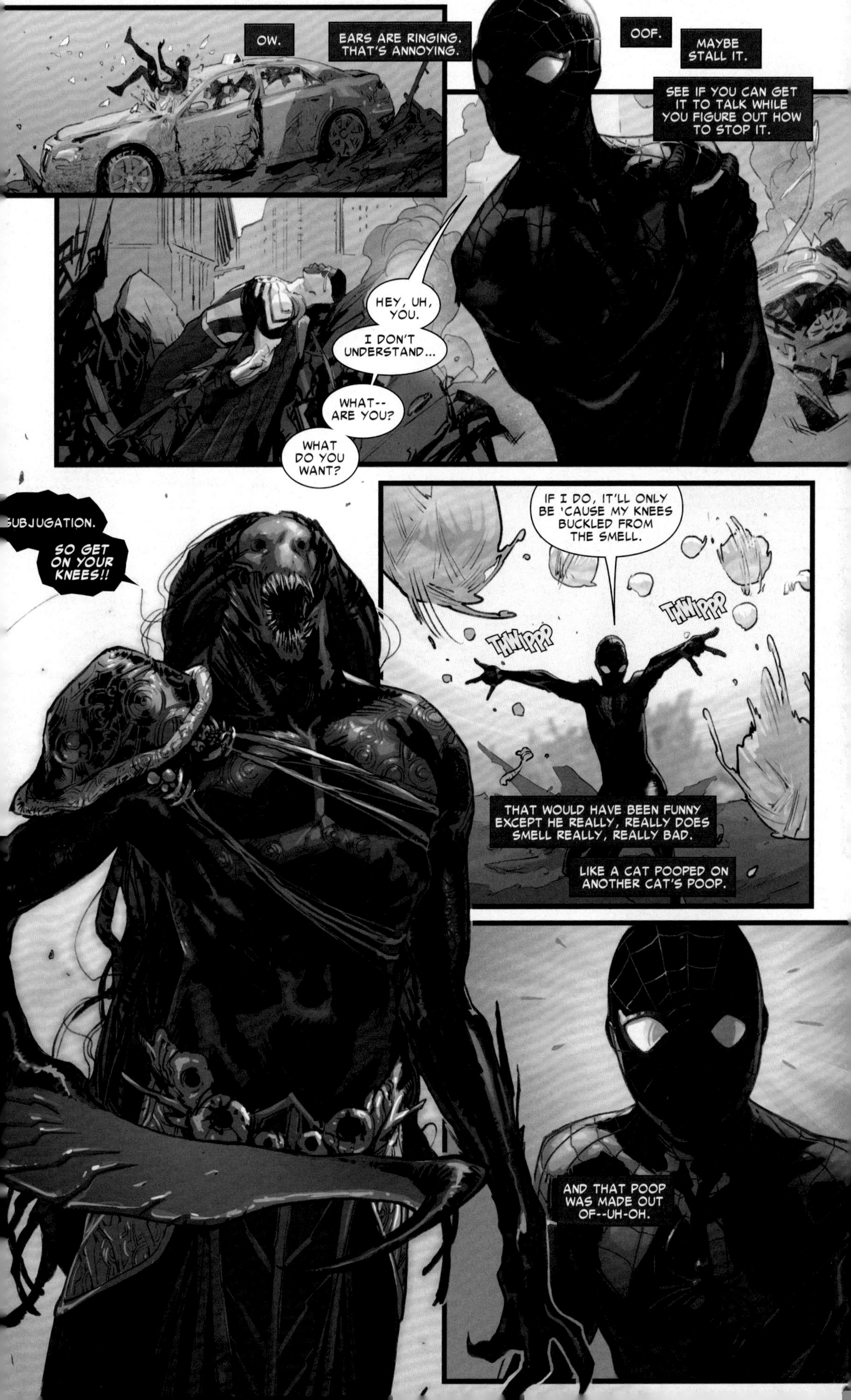

OW.
EARS ARE RINGING. THAT'S ANNOYING.
OOF.
MAYBE STALL IT.
SEE IF YOU CAN GET IT TO TALK WHILE YOU FIGURE OUT HOW TO STOP IT.
HEY, UH, YOU.
I DON'T UNDERSTAND...
WHAT-- ARE YOU?
WHAT DO YOU WANT?
SUBJUGATION.
SO GET ON YOUR KNEES!!
IF I DO, IT'LL ONLY BE 'CAUSE MY KNEES BUCKLED FROM THE SMELL.
THWIPPP
THWIPPP
THAT WOULD HAVE BEEN FUNNY EXCEPT HE REALLY, REALLY DOES SMELL REALLY, REALLY BAD.
LIKE A CAT POOPED ON ANOTHER CAT'S POOP.
AND THAT POOP WAS MADE OUT OF--UH-OH.

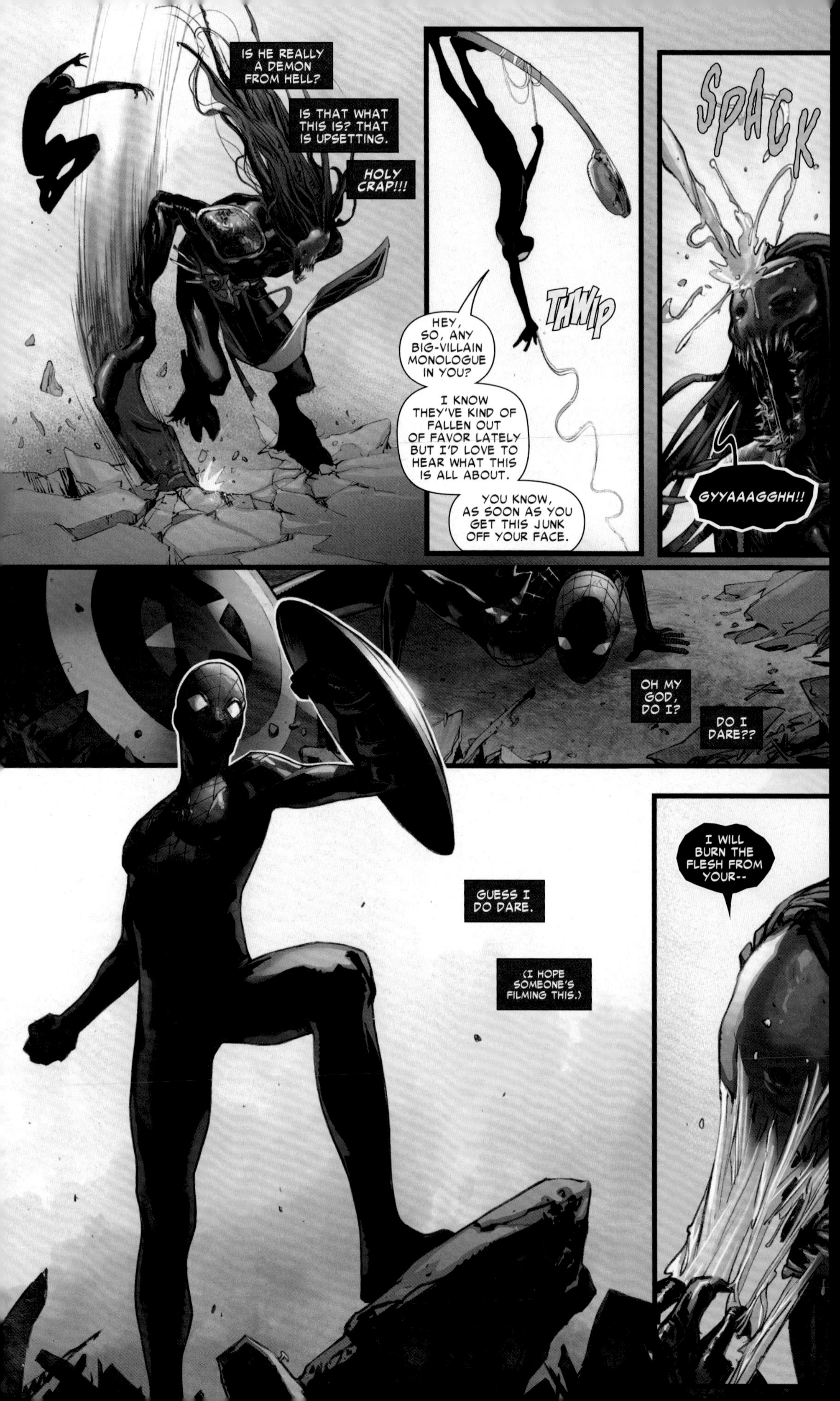
IS HE REALLY A DEMON FROM HELL?
IS THAT WHAT THIS IS? THAT IS UPSETTING.
HOLY CRAP!!!
HEY, SO, ANY BIG-VILLAIN MONOLOGUE IN YOU?
I KNOW THEY'VE KIND OF FALLEN OUT OF FAVOR LATELY BUT I'D LOVE TO HEAR WHAT THIS IS ALL ABOUT.
YOU KNOW, AS SOON AS YOU GET THIS JUNK OFF YOUR FACE.
THWIP
SPACK
GYYAAAGGHH!!
OH MY GOD, DO I?
DO I DARE??
GUESS I DO DARE.
(I HOPE SOMEONE'S FILMING THIS.)
I WILL BURN THE FLESH FROM YOUR--

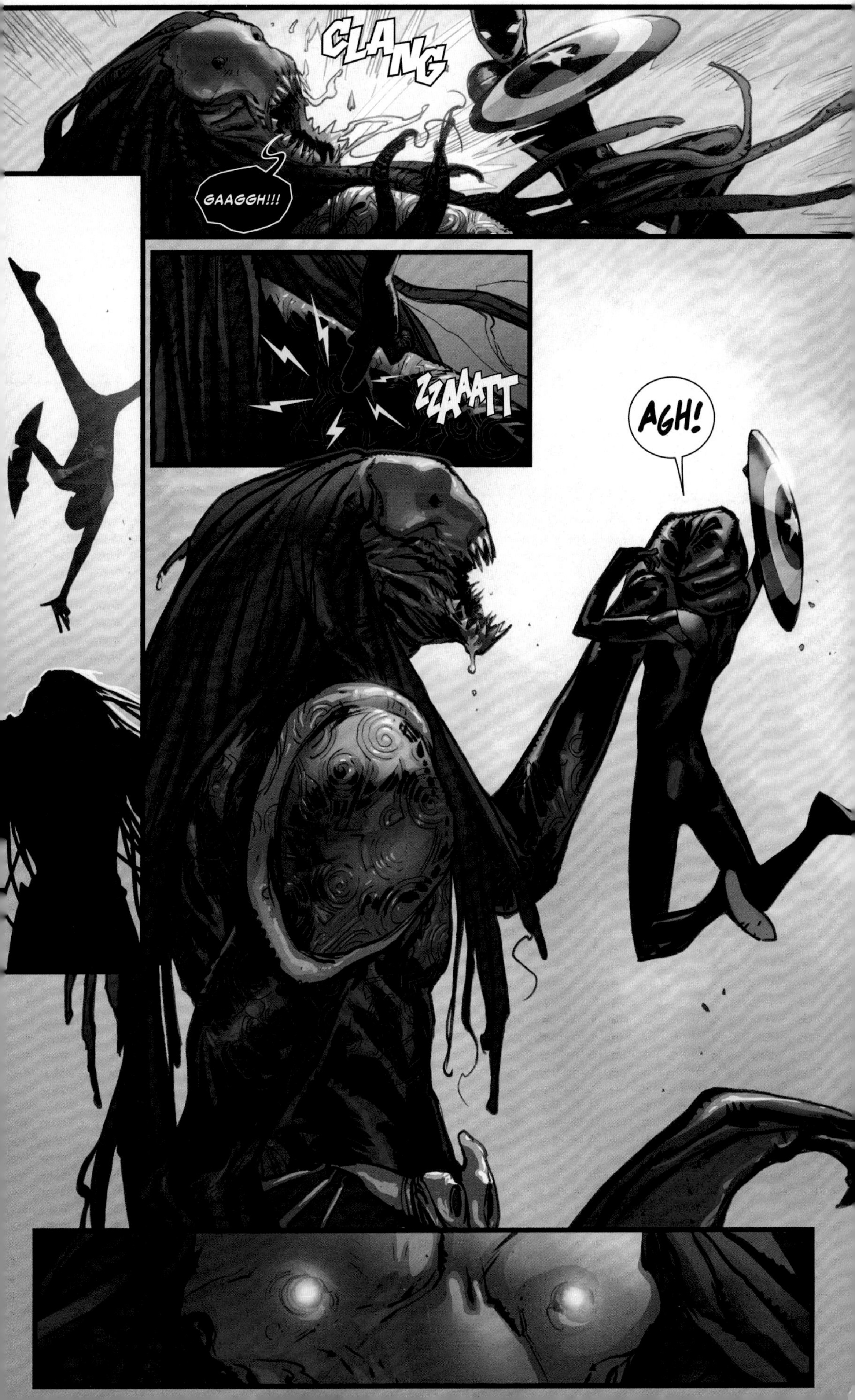
CLANG
GAAGGH!!!
ZZAAATT
AGH!

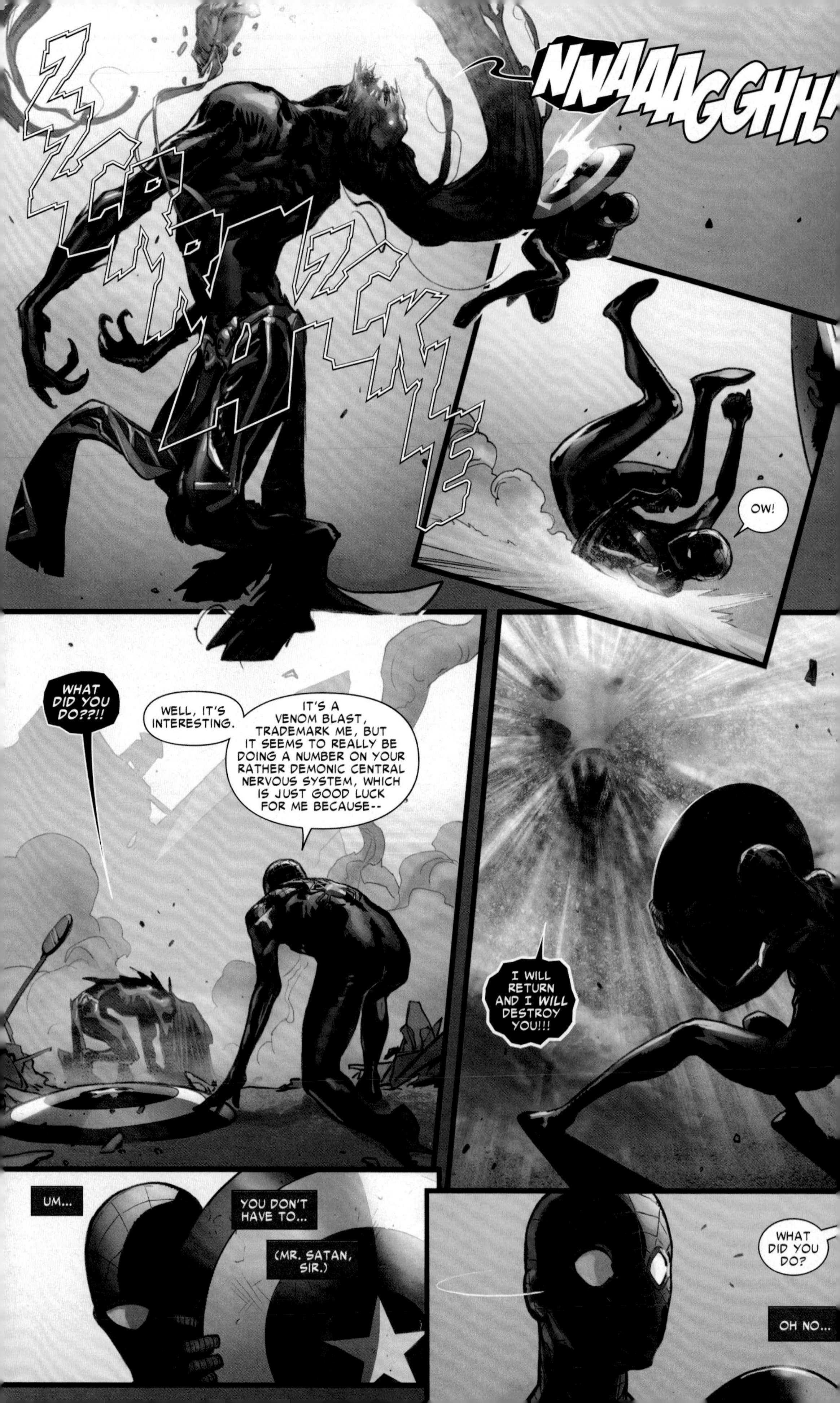

ZZRAKKK
NNAAAAGGHH!
OW!
WHAT DID YOU DO??!!
WELL, IT'S INTERESTING.
IT'S A VENOM BLAST, TRADEMARK ME, BUT IT SEEMS TO REALLY BE DOING A NUMBER ON YOUR RATHER DEMONIC CENTRAL NERVOUS SYSTEM, WHICH IS JUST GOOD LUCK FOR ME BECAUSE--
I WILL RETURN AND I *WILL* DESTROY YOU!!!
UM...
YOU DON'T HAVE TO...
(MR. SATAN, SIR.)
WHAT DID YOU DO?
OH NO...

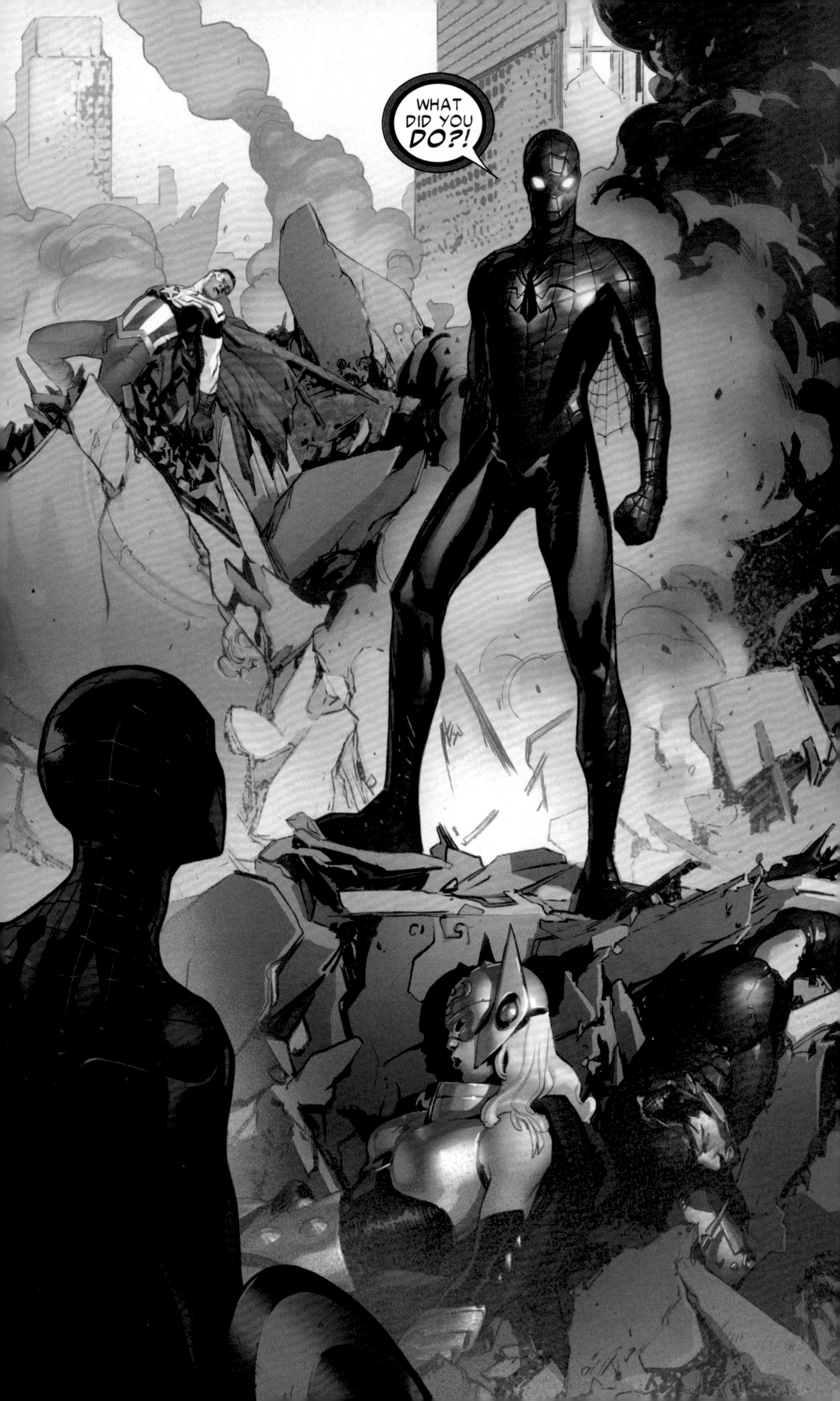
WHAT DID YOU DO?!

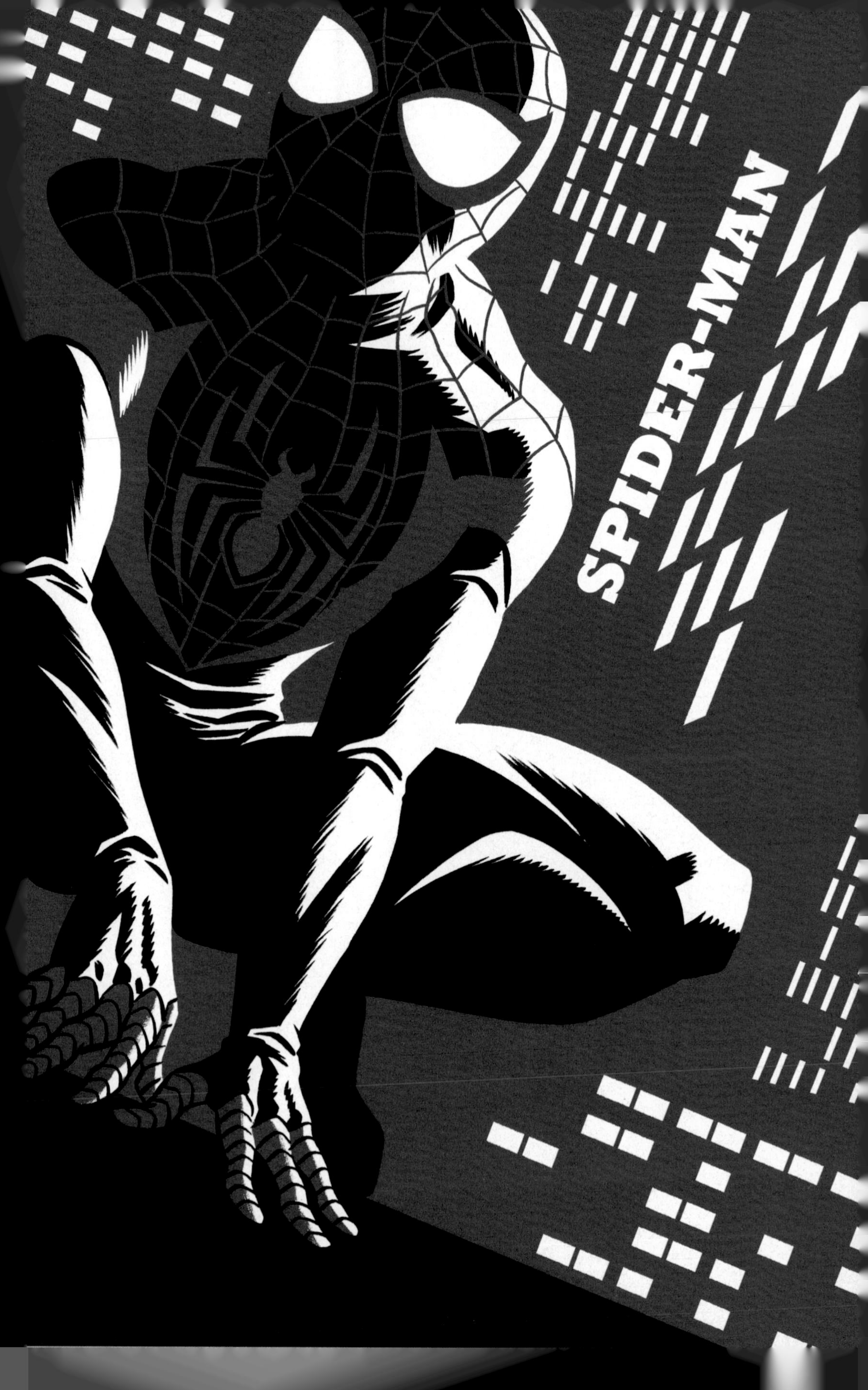
SPIDER-MAN

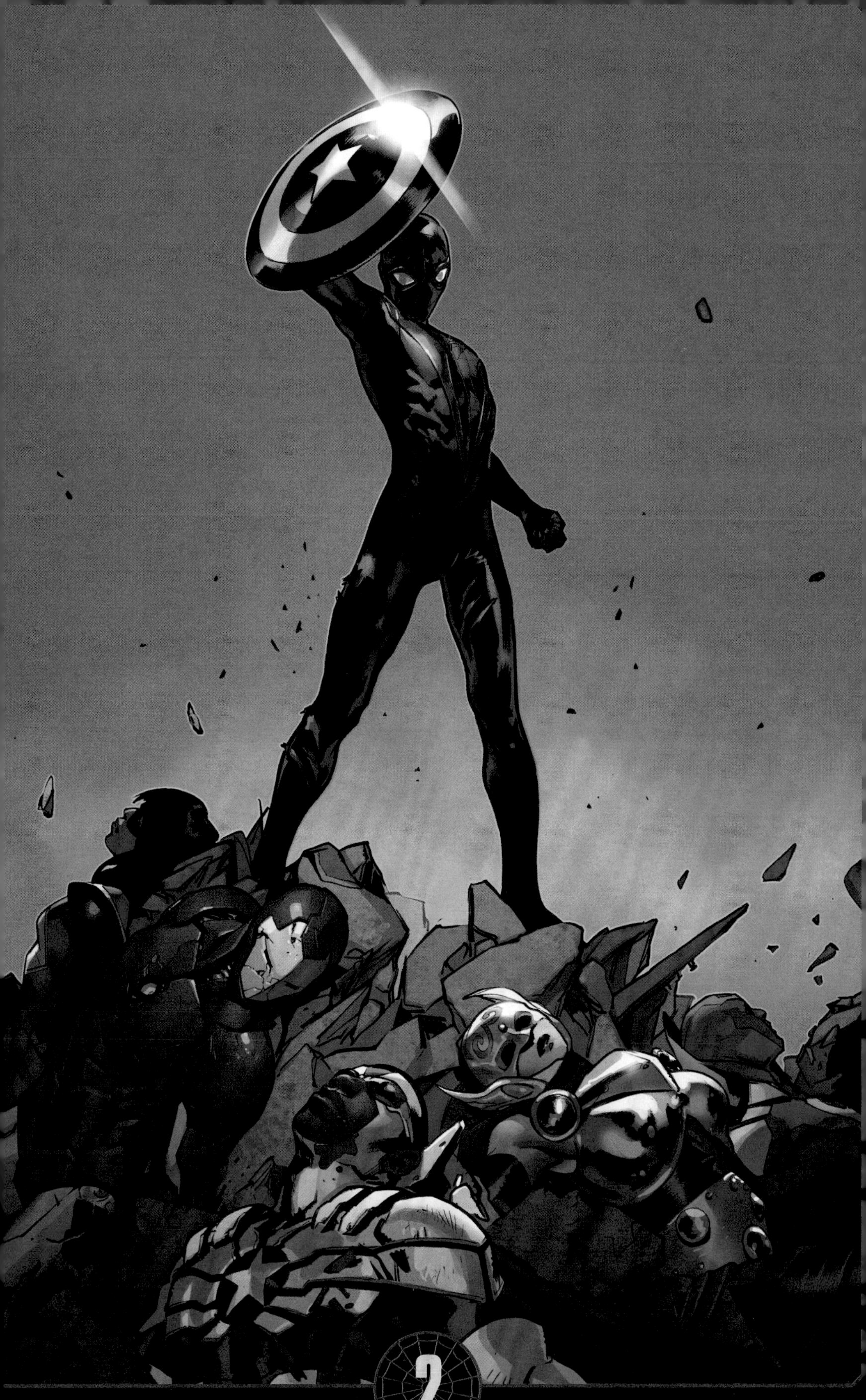

2

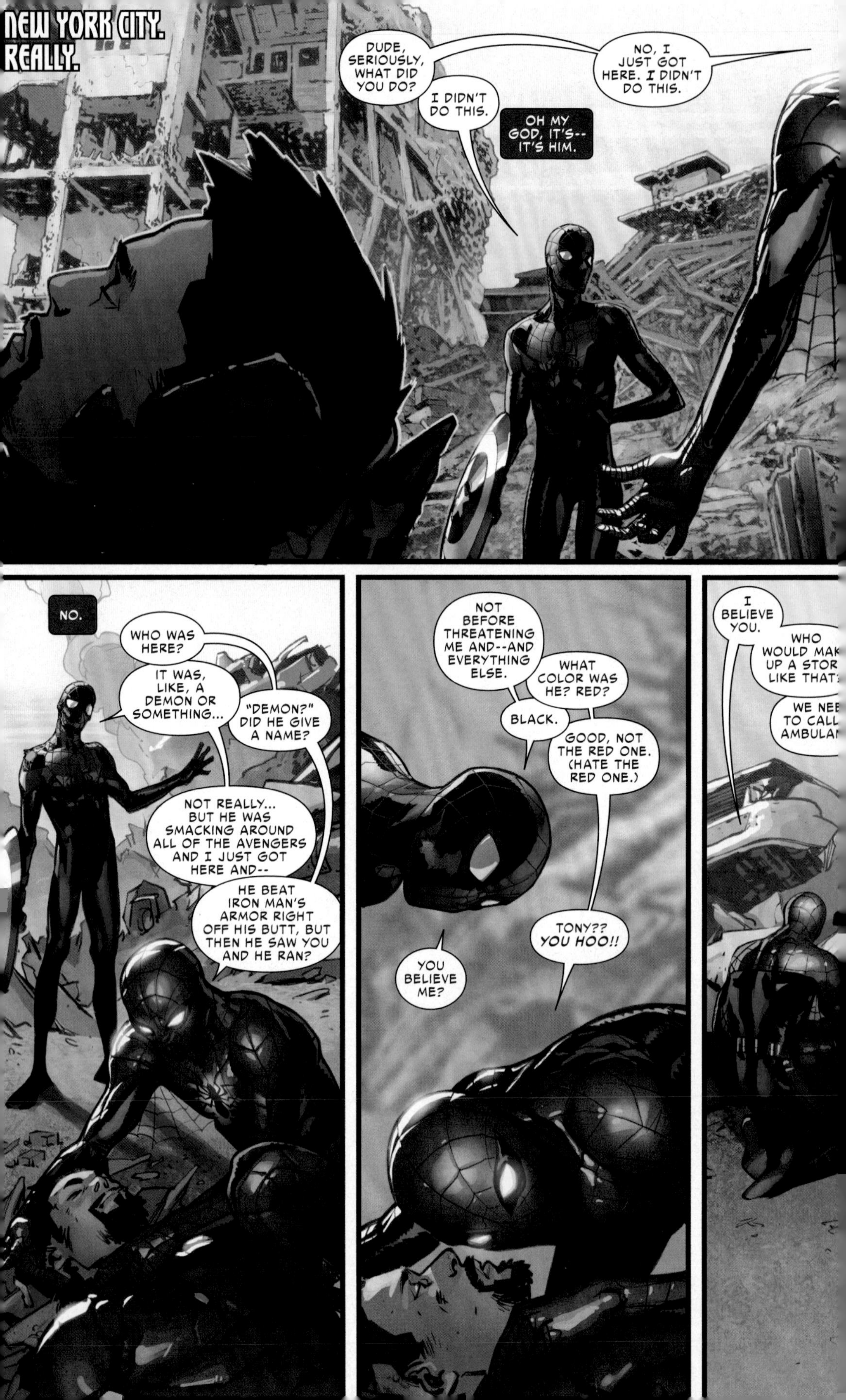

NEW YORK CITY. REALLY.
DUDE, SERIOUSLY, WHAT DID YOU DO?
NO, I JUST GOT HERE. *I* DIDN'T DO THIS.
I DIDN'T DO THIS.
OH MY GOD, IT'S-- IT'S HIM.
NO.
WHO WAS HERE?
IT WAS, LIKE, A DEMON OR SOMETHING...
"DEMON?" DID HE GIVE A NAME?
NOT REALLY... BUT HE WAS SMACKING AROUND ALL OF THE AVENGERS AND I JUST GOT HERE AND--
HE BEAT IRON MAN'S ARMOR RIGHT OFF HIS BUTT, BUT THEN HE SAW YOU AND HE RAN?
NOT BEFORE THREATENING ME AND--AND EVERYTHING ELSE.
WHAT COLOR WAS HE? RED?
BLACK.
GOOD, NOT THE RED ONE. (HATE THE RED ONE.)
TONY?? *YOU HOO!!*
YOU BELIEVE ME?
I BELIEVE YOU.
WHO WOULD MAK UP A STOR LIKE THAT
WE NEE TO CALL AMBULAN

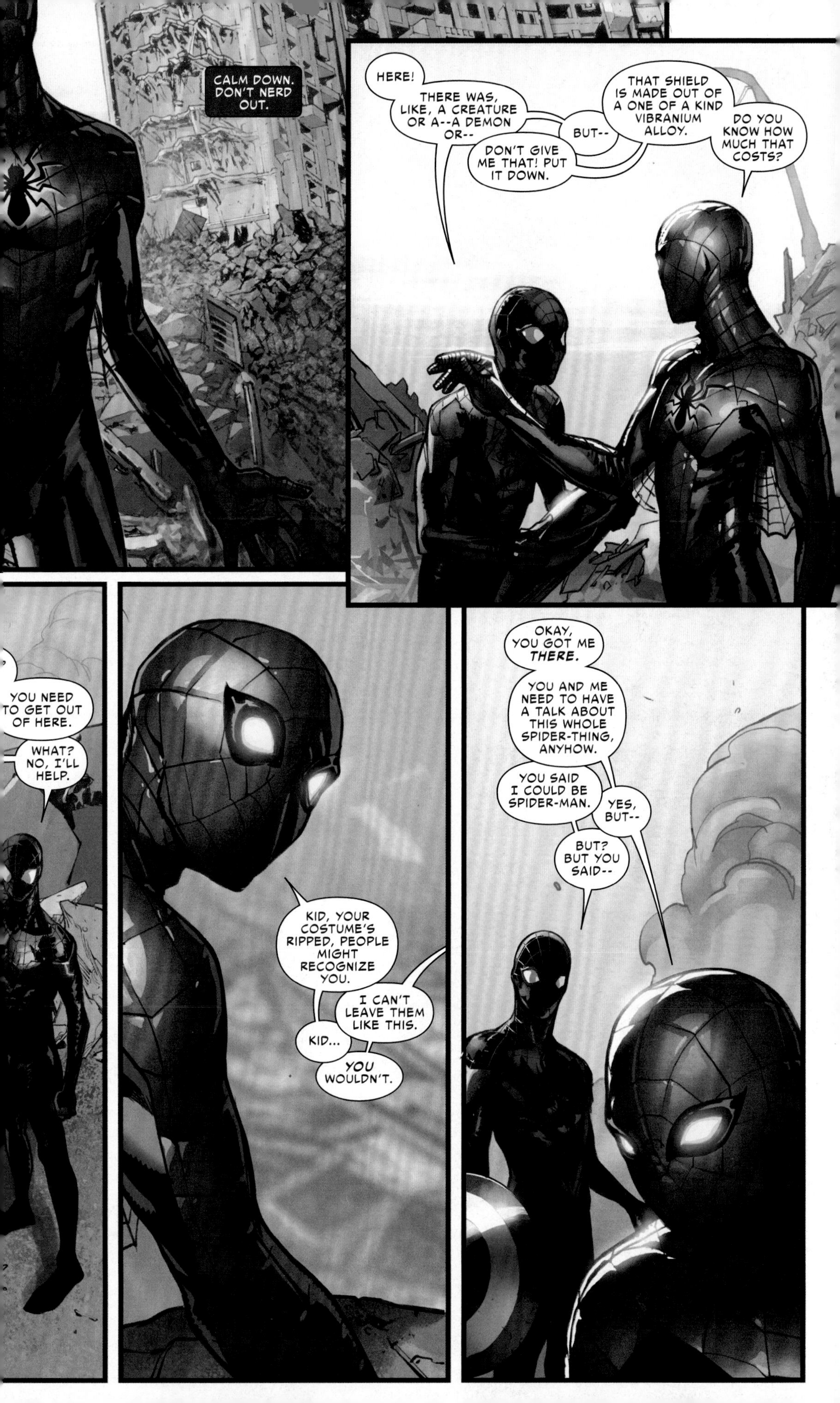
CALM DOWN. DON'T NERD OUT.
HERE!
THERE WAS, LIKE, A CREATURE OR A--A DEMON OR--
BUT--
DON'T GIVE ME THAT! PUT IT DOWN.
THAT SHIELD IS MADE OUT OF A ONE OF A KIND VIBRANIUM ALLOY.
DO YOU KNOW HOW MUCH THAT COSTS?
YOU NEED TO GET OUT OF HERE.
WHAT? NO, I'LL HELP.
KID, YOUR COSTUME'S RIPPED, PEOPLE MIGHT RECOGNIZE YOU.
I CAN'T LEAVE THEM LIKE THIS.
KID...
YOU WOULDN'T.
OKAY, YOU GOT ME THERE.
YOU AND ME NEED TO HAVE A TALK ABOUT THIS WHOLE SPIDER-THING, ANYHOW.
YOU SAID I COULD BE SPIDER-MAN.
YES, BUT--
BUT? BUT YOU SAID--

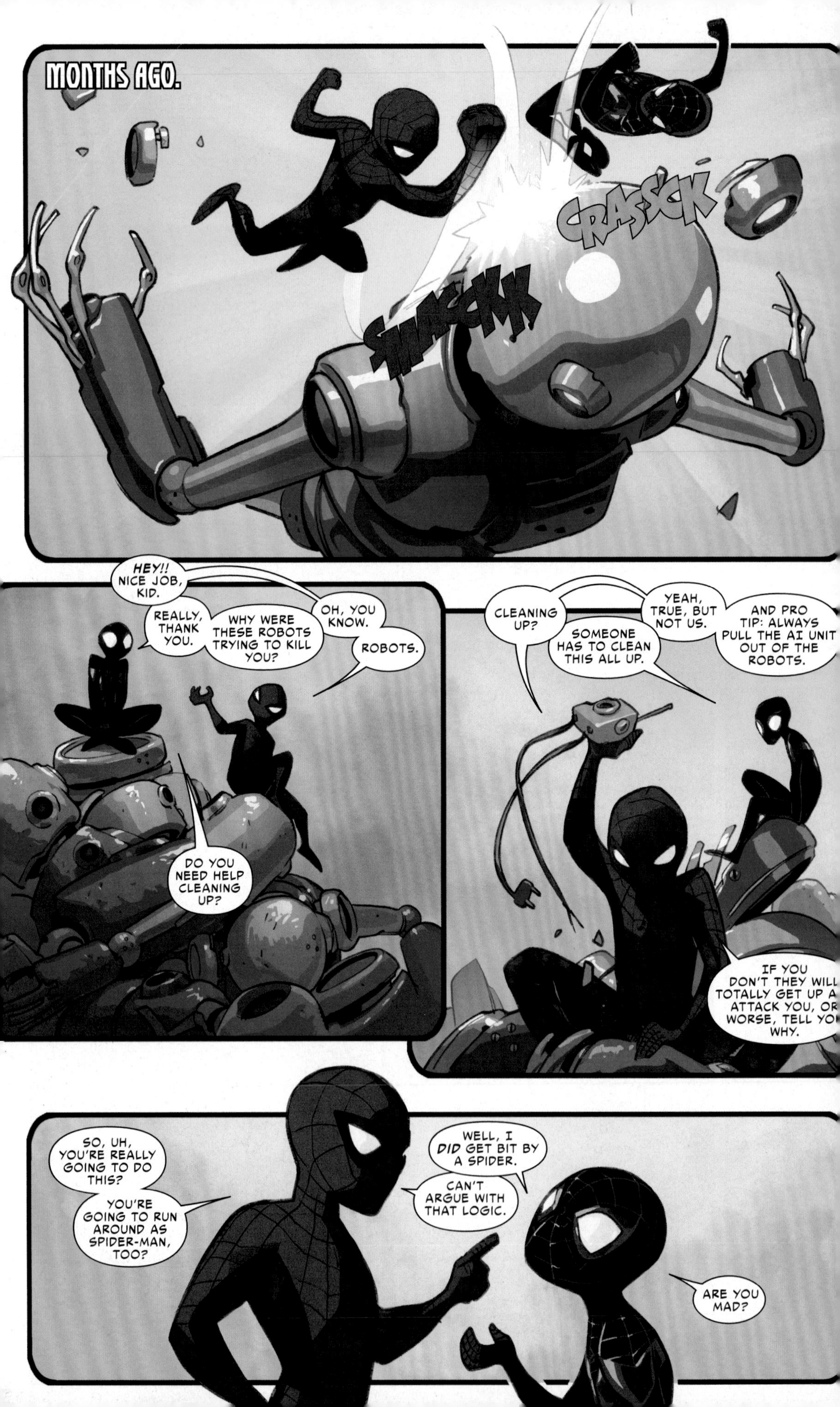

MONTHS AGO.
CRASSCK
SMASCKK
HEY!! NICE JOB, KID.
REALLY, THANK YOU.
WHY WERE THESE ROBOTS TRYING TO KILL YOU?
OH, YOU KNOW.
ROBOTS.
DO YOU NEED HELP CLEANING UP?
CLEANING UP?
SOMEONE HAS TO CLEAN THIS ALL UP.
YEAH, TRUE, BUT NOT US.
AND PRO TIP: ALWAYS PULL THE AI UNIT OUT OF THE ROBOTS.
IF YOU DON'T THEY WILL TOTALLY GET UP A ATTACK YOU, OR WORSE, TELL YO WHY.
SO, UH, YOU'RE REALLY GOING TO DO THIS?
YOU'RE GOING TO RUN AROUND AS SPIDER-MAN, TOO?
WELL, I DID GET BIT BY A SPIDER.
CAN'T ARGUE WITH THAT LOGIC.
ARE YOU MAD?

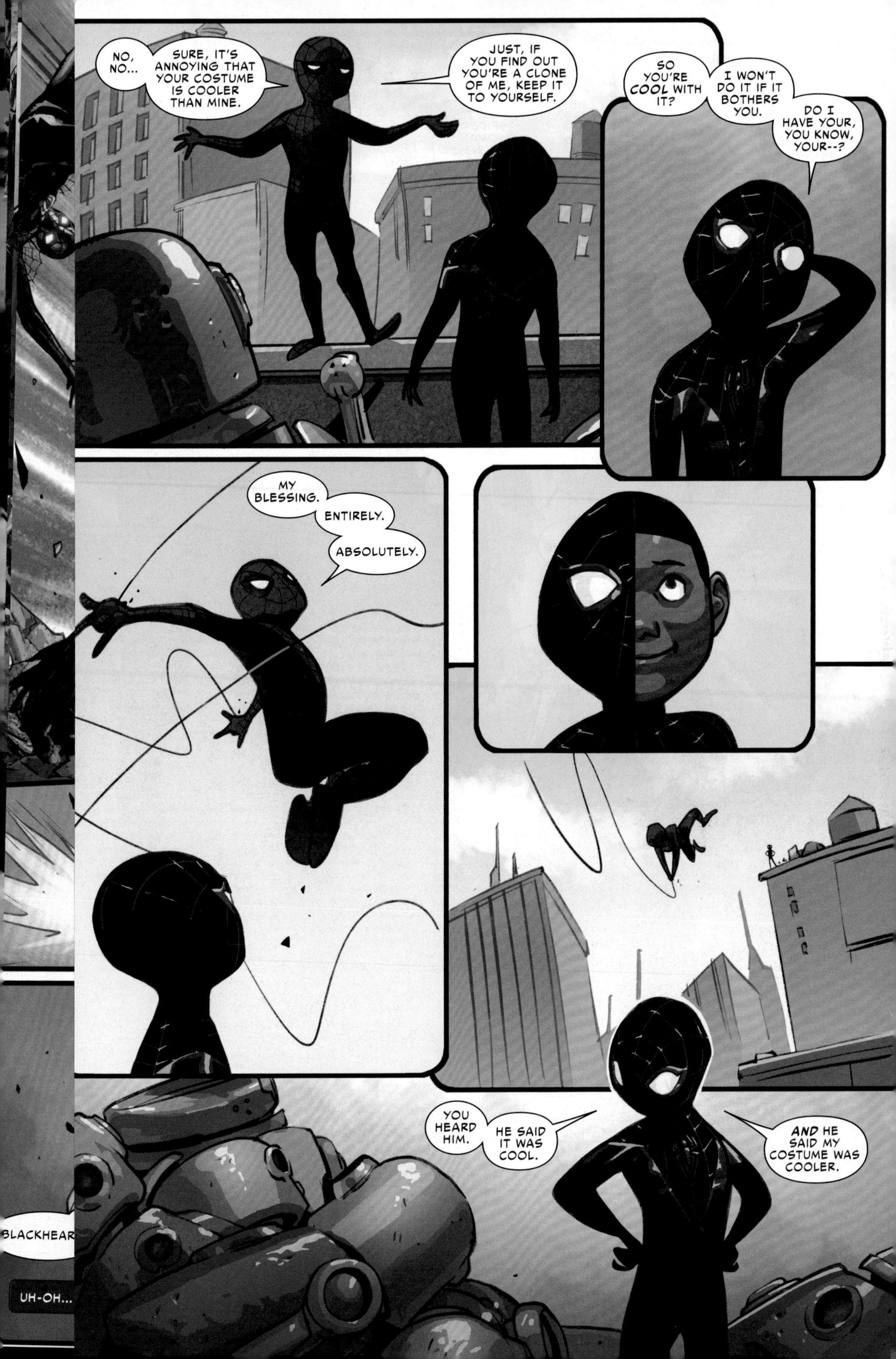
NO, NO...
SURE, IT'S ANNOYING THAT YOUR COSTUME IS COOLER THAN MINE.
JUST, IF YOU FIND OUT YOU'RE A CLONE OF ME, KEEP IT TO YOURSELF.
SO YOU'RE COOL WITH IT?
I WON'T DO IT IF IT BOTHERS YOU.
DO I HAVE YOUR, YOU KNOW, YOUR--?
MY BLESSING.
ENTIRELY.
ABSOLUTELY.
YOU HEARD HIM.
HE SAID IT WAS COOL.
AND HE SAID MY COSTUME WAS COOLER.
BLACKHEAR
UH-OH...

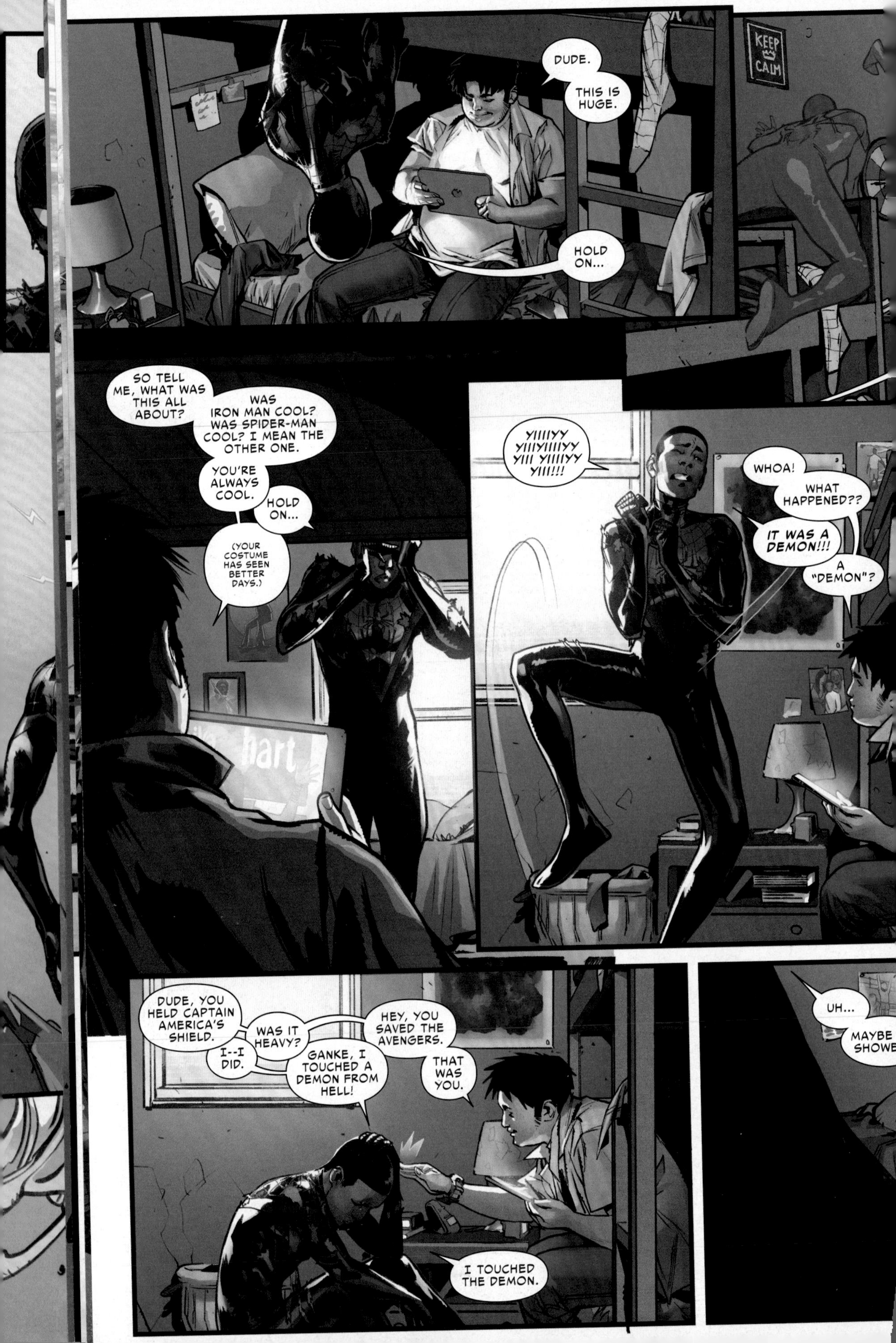
KEEP CALM
DUDE.
THIS IS HUGE.
HOLD ON...
SO TELL ME, WHAT WAS THIS ALL ABOUT?
WAS IRON MAN COOL? WAS SPIDER-MAN COOL? I MEAN THE OTHER ONE.
YOU'RE ALWAYS COOL.
HOLD ON...
(YOUR COSTUME HAS SEEN BETTER DAYS.)
YIIIIYY YIIIYIIIIYY YIII YIIIIYY YIII!!!
WHOA!
WHAT HAPPENED??
IT WAS A DEMON!!!
A "DEMON"?
DUDE, YOU HELD CAPTAIN AMERICA'S SHIELD.
I--I DID.
WAS IT HEAVY?
GANKE, I TOUCHED A DEMON FROM HELL!
HEY, YOU SAVED THE AVENGERS.
THAT WAS YOU.
I TOUCHED THE DEMON.
UH...
MAYBE SHOWE

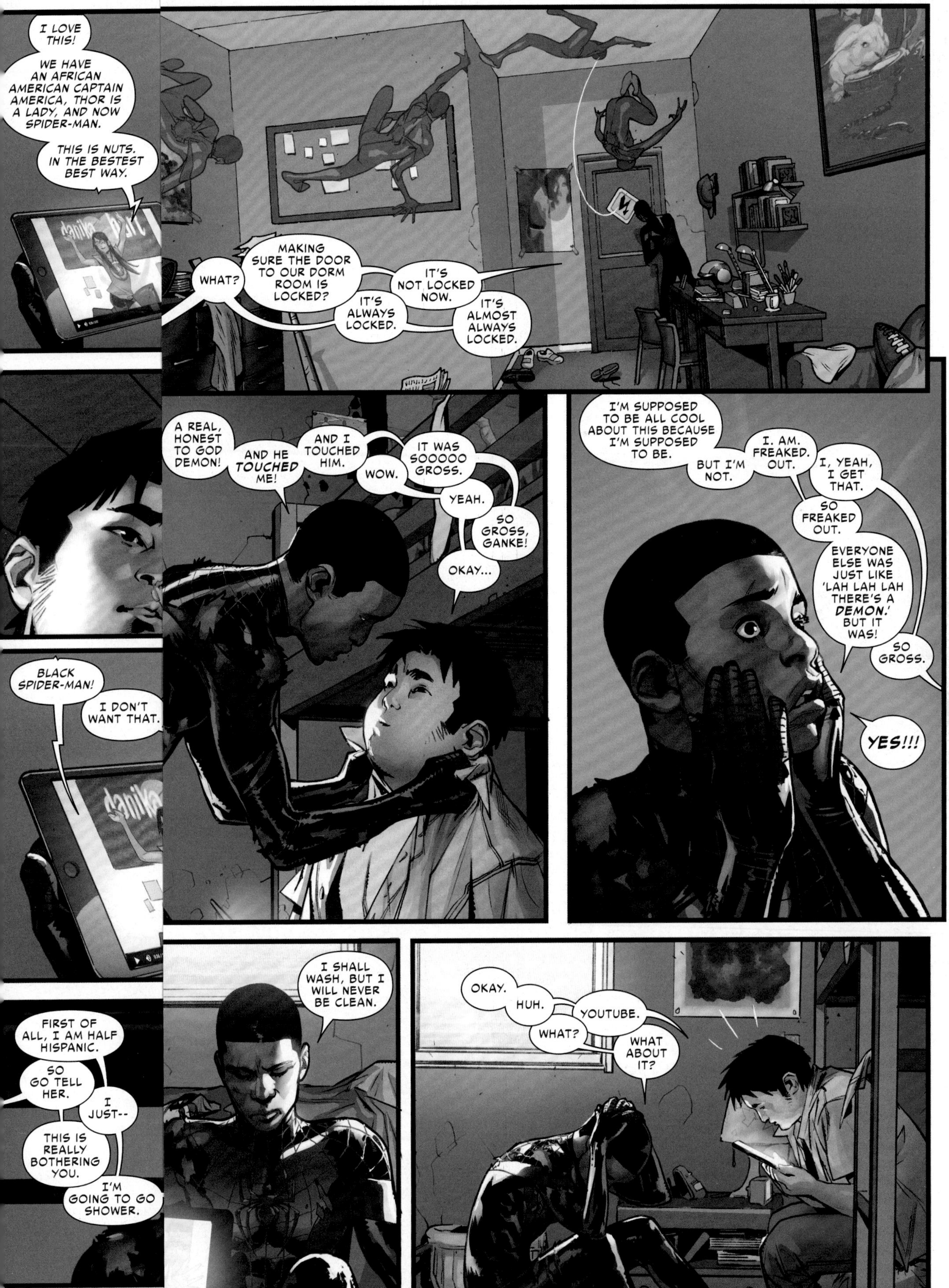

I LOVE THIS!
WE HAVE AN AFRICAN AMERICAN CAPTAIN AMERICA, THOR IS A LADY, AND NOW SPIDER-MAN.
THIS IS NUTS. IN THE BESTEST BEST WAY.
WHAT?
MAKING SURE THE DOOR TO OUR DORM ROOM IS LOCKED?
IT'S NOT LOCKED NOW.
IT'S ALWAYS LOCKED.
IT'S ALMOST ALWAYS LOCKED.
A REAL, HONEST TO GOD DEMON!
AND HE *TOUCHED* ME!
AND I TOUCHED HIM.
IT WAS SOOOOO GROSS.
WOW.
YEAH.
SO GROSS, GANKE!
OKAY...
I'M SUPPOSED TO BE ALL COOL ABOUT THIS BECAUSE I'M SUPPOSED TO BE.
BUT I'M NOT.
I. AM. FREAKED. OUT.
I, YEAH, I GET THAT.
SO FREAKED OUT.
EVERYONE ELSE WAS JUST LIKE 'LAH LAH LAH THERE'S A *DEMON.*' BUT IT WAS!
SO GROSS.
YES!!!
BLACK SPIDER-MAN!
I DON'T WANT THAT.
FIRST OF ALL, I AM HALF HISPANIC.
SO GO TELL HER.
I JUST--
THIS IS REALLY BOTHERING YOU.
I'M GOING TO GO SHOWER.
I SHALL WASH, BUT I WILL NEVER BE CLEAN.
OKAY.
HUH.
YOUTUBE.
WHAT?
WHAT ABOUT IT?

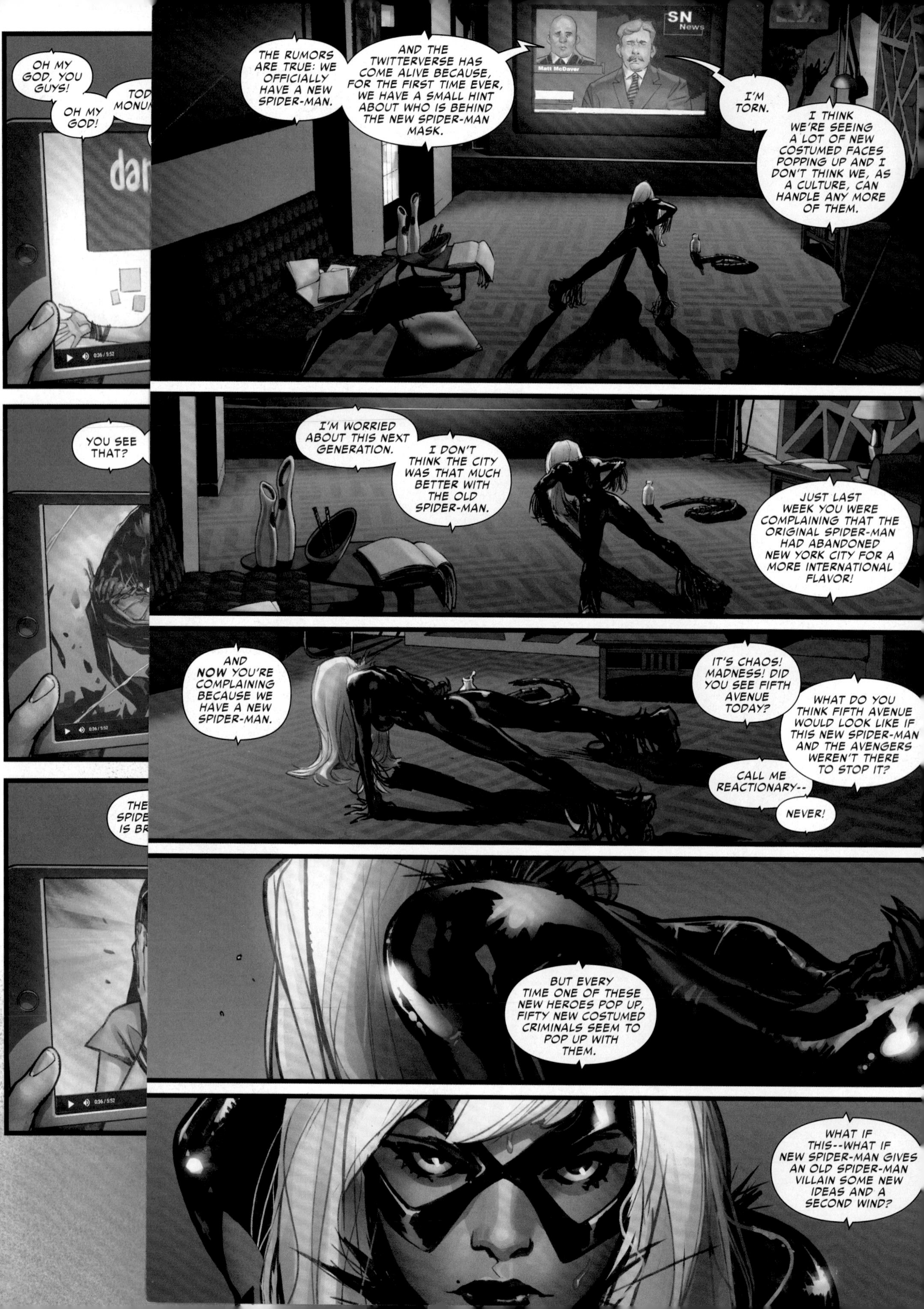
OH MY GOD, YOU GUYS!
OH MY GOD!
YOU SEE THAT?
SN News
Matt McDover
THE RUMORS ARE TRUE: WE OFFICIALLY HAVE A NEW SPIDER-MAN.
AND THE TWITTERVERSE HAS COME ALIVE BECAUSE, FOR THE FIRST TIME EVER, WE HAVE A SMALL HINT ABOUT WHO IS BEHIND THE NEW SPIDER-MAN MASK.
I'M TORN.
I THINK WE'RE SEEING A LOT OF NEW COSTUMED FACES POPPING UP AND I DON'T THINK WE, AS A CULTURE, CAN HANDLE ANY MORE OF THEM.
I'M WORRIED ABOUT THIS NEXT GENERATION.
I DON'T THINK THE CITY WAS THAT MUCH BETTER WITH THE OLD SPIDER-MAN.
JUST LAST WEEK YOU WERE COMPLAINING THAT THE ORIGINAL SPIDER-MAN HAD ABANDONED NEW YORK CITY FOR A MORE INTERNATIONAL FLAVOR!
AND NOW YOU'RE COMPLAINING BECAUSE WE HAVE A NEW SPIDER-MAN.
IT'S CHAOS! MADNESS! DID YOU SEE FIFTH AVENUE TODAY?
WHAT DO YOU THINK FIFTH AVENUE WOULD LOOK LIKE IF THIS NEW SPIDER-MAN AND THE AVENGERS WEREN'T THERE TO STOP IT?
CALL ME REACTIONARY--
NEVER!
BUT EVERY TIME ONE OF THESE NEW HEROES POP UP, FIFTY NEW COSTUMED CRIMINALS SEEM TO POP UP WITH THEM.
WHAT IF THIS--WHAT IF NEW SPIDER-MAN GIVES AN OLD SPIDER-MAN VILLAIN SOME NEW IDEAS AND A SECOND WIND?

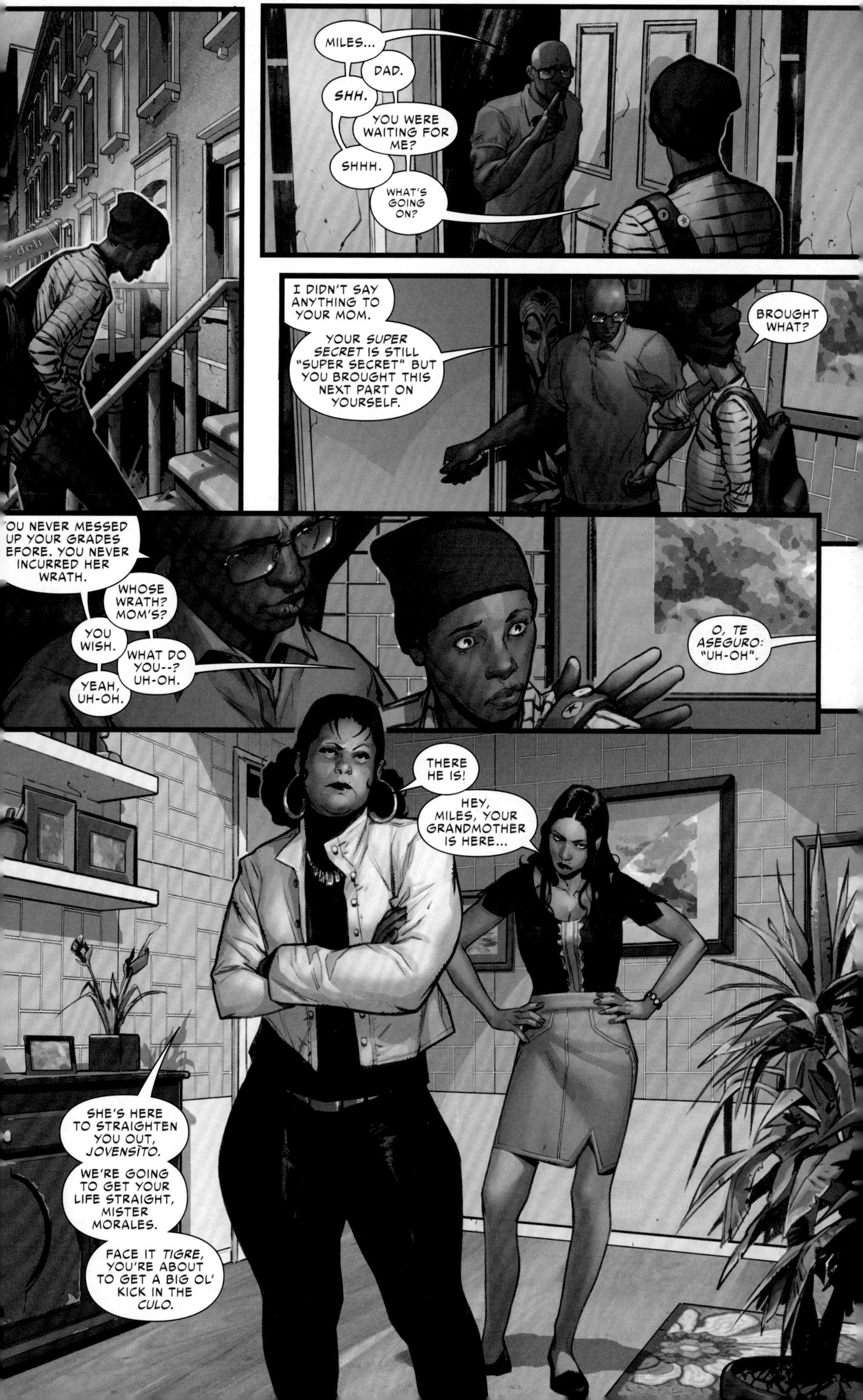
MILES...
DAD.
SHH.
YOU WERE WAITING FOR ME?
SHHH.
WHAT'S GOING ON?
I DIDN'T SAY ANYTHING TO YOUR MOM.
YOUR SUPER SECRET IS STILL "SUPER SECRET" BUT YOU BROUGHT THIS NEXT PART ON YOURSELF.
BROUGHT WHAT?
OU NEVER MESSED UP YOUR GRADES EFORE. YOU NEVER INCURRED HER WRATH.
WHOSE WRATH? MOM'S?
YOU WISH.
WHAT DO YOU--? UH-OH.
YEAH, UH-OH.
O, TE ASEGURO: "UH-OH".
THERE HE IS!
HEY, MILES, YOUR GRANDMOTHER IS HERE...
SHE'S HERE TO STRAIGHTEN YOU OUT, JOVENSITO.
WE'RE GOING TO GET YOUR LIFE STRAIGHT, MISTER MORALES.
FACE IT TIGRE, YOU'RE ABOUT TO GET A BIG OL' KICK IN THE CULO.

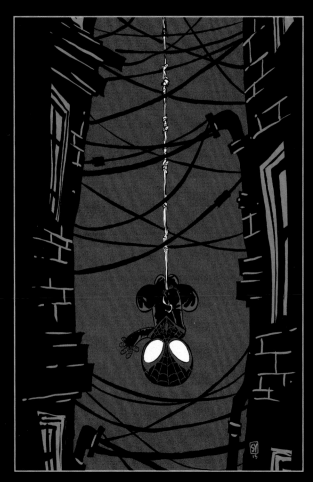

SKOTTIE YOUNG
1 VARIANT

MARK BAGLEY,
DEXTER VINES &
ANDREW CROSSLEY
1 VARIANT

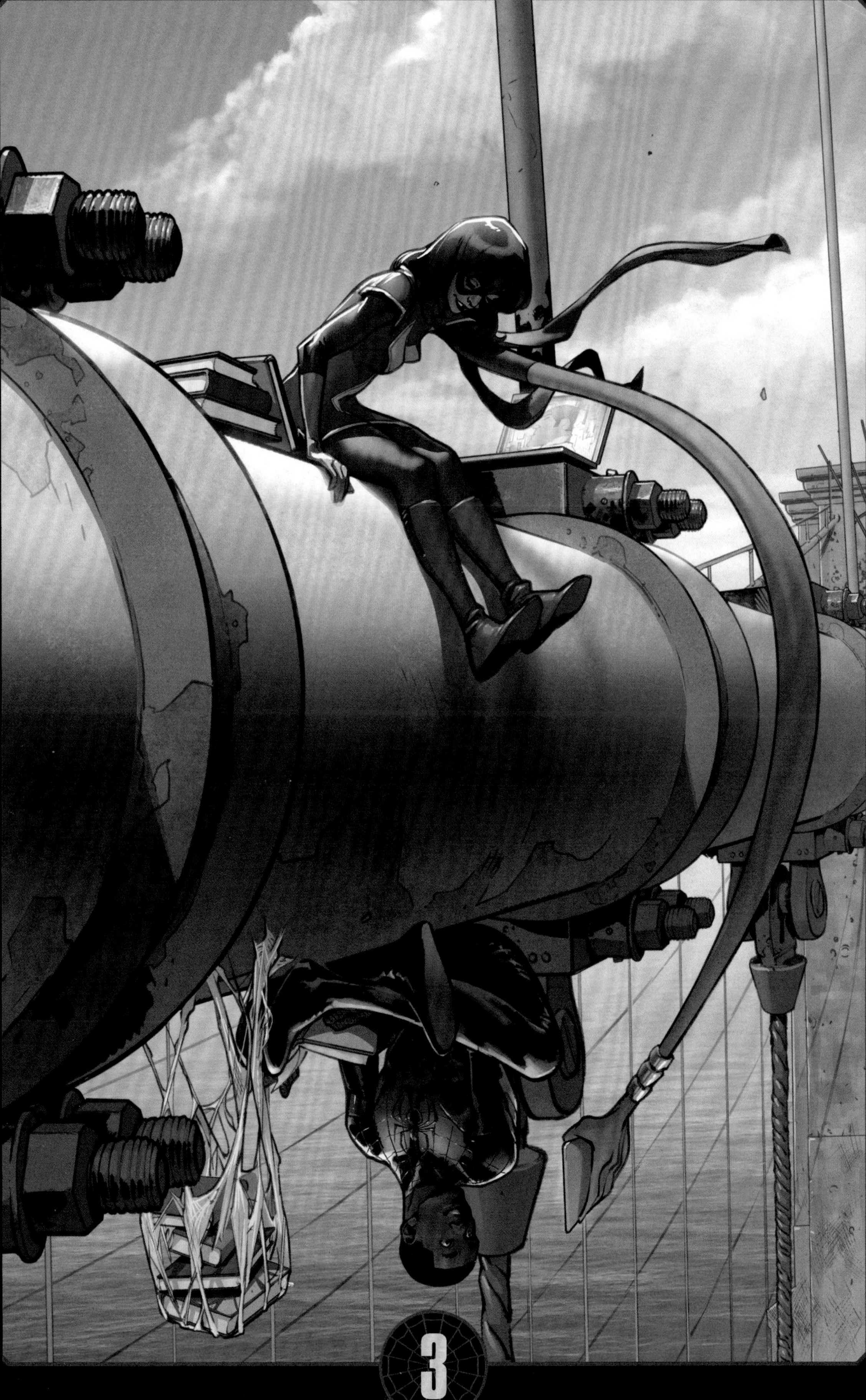
3

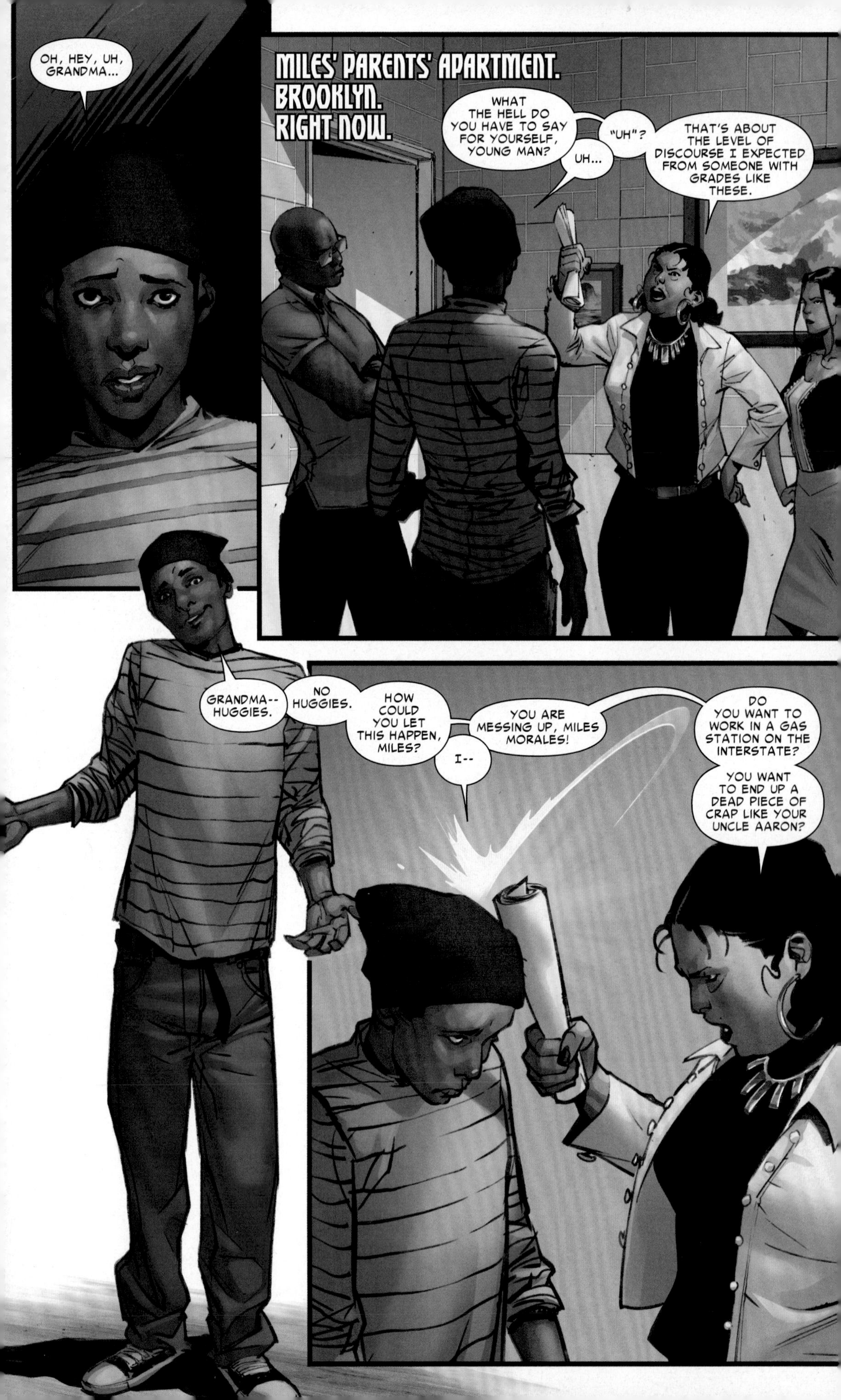
OH, HEY, UH, GRANDMA...
MILES' PARENTS' APARTMENT. BROOKLYN. RIGHT NOW.
WHAT THE HELL DO YOU HAVE TO SAY FOR YOURSELF, YOUNG MAN?
UH...
"UH"?
THAT'S ABOUT THE LEVEL OF DISCOURSE I EXPECTED FROM SOMEONE WITH GRADES LIKE THESE.
GRANDMA-- HUGGIES.
NO HUGGIES.
HOW COULD YOU LET THIS HAPPEN, MILES?
I--
YOU ARE MESSING UP, MILES MORALES!
DO YOU WANT TO WORK IN A GAS STATION ON THE INTERSTATE?
YOU WANT TO END UP A DEAD PIECE OF CRAP LIKE YOUR UNCLE AARON?

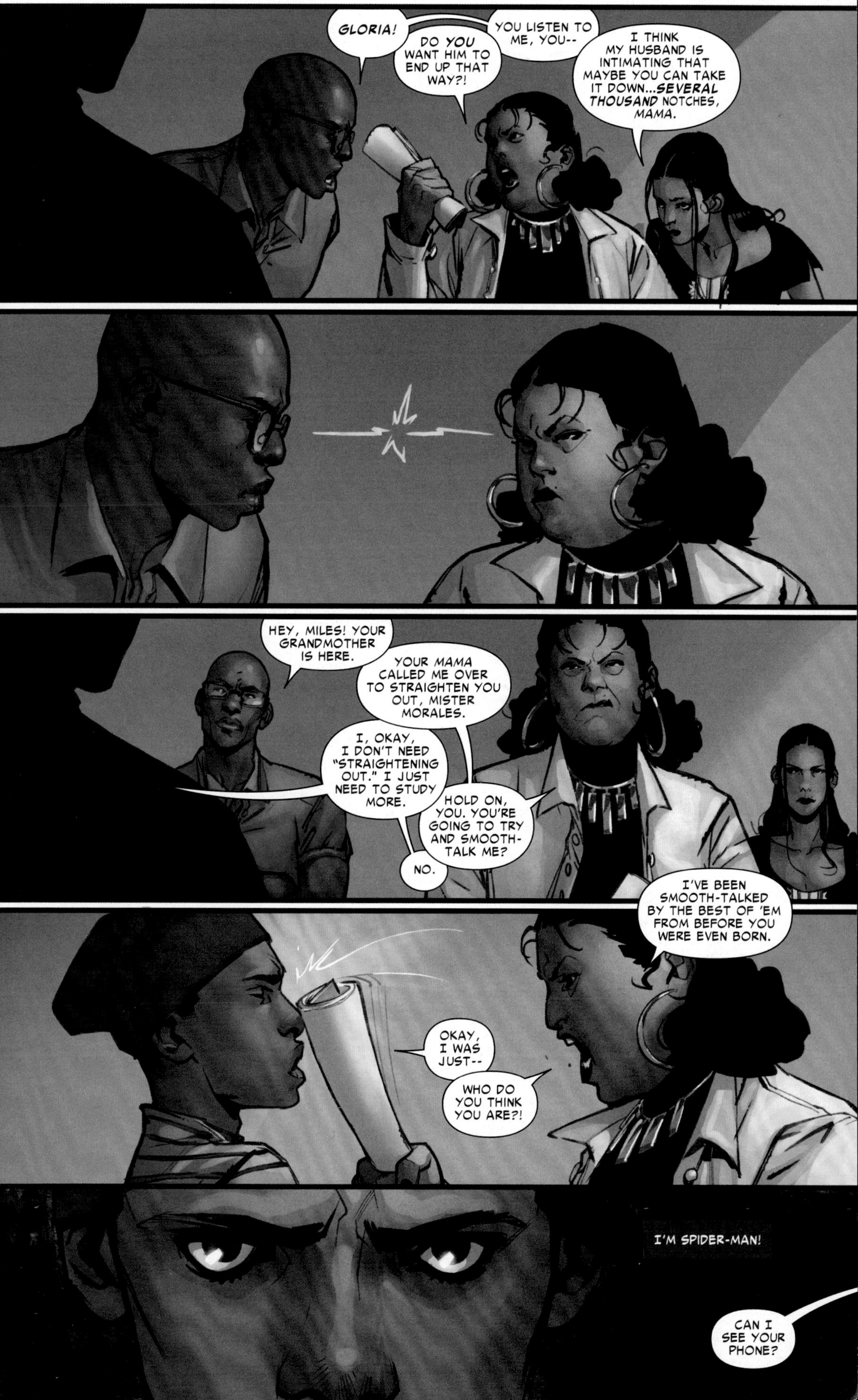
GLORIA!
YOU LISTEN TO ME, YOU--
DO YOU WANT HIM TO END UP THAT WAY?!
I THINK MY HUSBAND IS INTIMATING THAT MAYBE YOU CAN TAKE IT DOWN...SEVERAL THOUSAND NOTCHES, MAMA.
HEY, MILES! YOUR GRANDMOTHER IS HERE.
YOUR MAMA CALLED ME OVER TO STRAIGHTEN YOU OUT, MISTER MORALES.
I, OKAY, I DON'T NEED "STRAIGHTENING OUT." I JUST NEED TO STUDY MORE.
HOLD ON, YOU. YOU'RE GOING TO TRY AND SMOOTH-TALK ME?
NO.
I'VE BEEN SMOOTH-TALKED BY THE BEST OF 'EM FROM BEFORE YOU WERE EVEN BORN.
OKAY, I WAS JUST--
WHO DO YOU THINK YOU ARE?!
I'M SPIDER-MAN!
CAN I SEE YOUR PHONE?

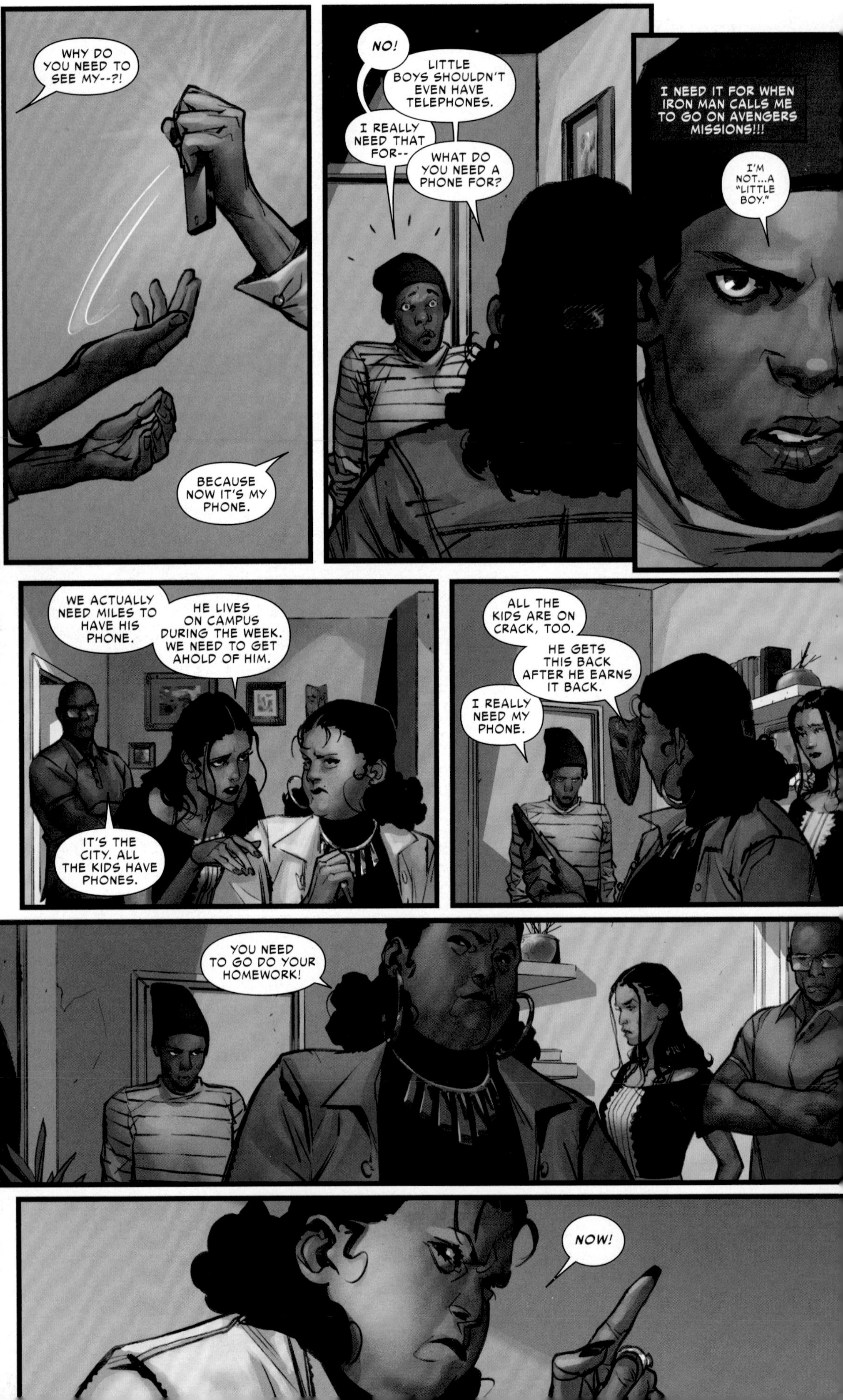
WHY DO YOU NEED TO SEE MY--?!
BECAUSE NOW IT'S MY PHONE.
NO!
LITTLE BOYS SHOULDN'T EVEN HAVE TELEPHONES.
I REALLY NEED THAT FOR--
WHAT DO YOU NEED A PHONE FOR?
I NEED IT FOR WHEN IRON MAN CALLS ME TO GO ON AVENGERS MISSIONS!!!
I'M NOT...A "LITTLE BOY."
WE ACTUALLY NEED MILES TO HAVE HIS PHONE.
HE LIVES ON CAMPUS DURING THE WEEK. WE NEED TO GET AHOLD OF HIM.
IT'S THE CITY. ALL THE KIDS HAVE PHONES.
ALL THE KIDS ARE ON CRACK, TOO.
HE GETS THIS BACK AFTER HE EARNS IT BACK.
I REALLY NEED MY PHONE.
YOU NEED TO GO DO YOUR HOMEWORK!
NOW!

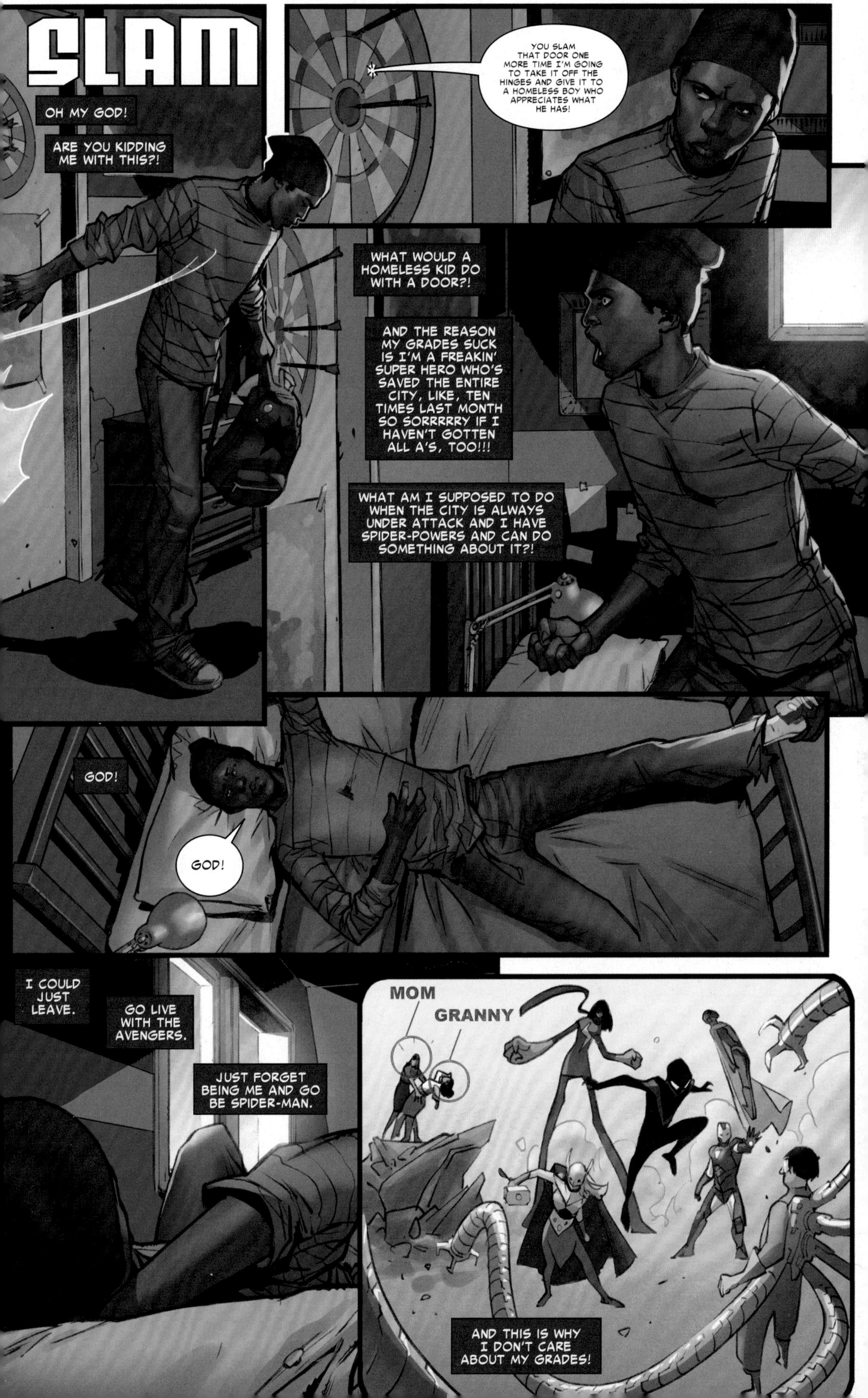
SLAM
OH MY GOD!
ARE YOU KIDDING ME WITH THIS?!
YOU SLAM THAT DOOR ONE MORE TIME I'M GOING TO TAKE IT OFF THE HINGES AND GIVE IT TO A HOMELESS BOY WHO APPRECIATES WHAT HE HAS!
WHAT WOULD A HOMELESS KID DO WITH A DOOR?!
AND THE REASON MY GRADES SUCK IS I'M A FREAKIN' SUPER HERO WHO'S SAVED THE ENTIRE CITY, LIKE, TEN TIMES LAST MONTH SO SORRRRRY IF I HAVEN'T GOTTEN ALL A'S, TOO!!!
WHAT AM I SUPPOSED TO DO WHEN THE CITY IS ALWAYS UNDER ATTACK AND I HAVE SPIDER-POWERS AND CAN DO SOMETHING ABOUT IT?!
GOD!
GOD!
I COULD JUST LEAVE.
GO LIVE WITH THE AVENGERS.
JUST FORGET BEING ME AND GO BE SPIDER-MAN.
MOM
GRANNY
AND THIS IS WHY I DON'T CARE ABOUT MY GRADES!

AAAAAND THEN MY MOM KEELS OVER FROM SHOCK AND DIES.

MY GRANDMOTHER WILL PROBABLY OUT ME TO THE PRESS TO SHOW ME WHO'S BOSS AND, MAN, WHAT IS WITH MY DAD NOT STANDING UP TO GRANDMA?

GROW A PAIR, DUDE.

GUY USED TO BE A BAD-ASS GANGSTER, NOW HE CAN'T EVEN GET MY PHONE OUT OF MY GRANDMA'S HAND.

THANK GOD I LOCKED MY PHONE AND HAVE ALL MY SECRET SUPER HERO NUMBERS UNDER CODENAMES.

WHAT IF IRON MAN CALLS? WHAT IF MS. MARVEL CALLS?

WHAT IF GANKE CALLS?

HE'S GOING TO BE SO WORRIED IF HE CAN'T GET ME ON THE-- I CAN'T BELIEVE I WAS ACTUALLY ABOUT TO THINK THAT.

LITTLE OVER THE TOP, DON'T YOU THINK?

HE DISCOVERED GIRLS.

GIRLS WITH DRUGS.

MOM.

YOU CALLED ME DOWN HERE TO SCARE HIM STRAIGHT.

YES, YES, I DID.

YOU'RE WELCOME.

I'M GOING TO THE BATHROOM.

YOU THINK IT'S CUTE, BUT I THINK SHE'S TRULY MENTALLY ILL.

I DIDN'T KNOW WHAT ELSE TO DO.

YOU KNOW THE TOP REASO I LOVE YOU IS BECAUSE YOU RO ABOVE BEING RAISED BY THAT.

DING DONG

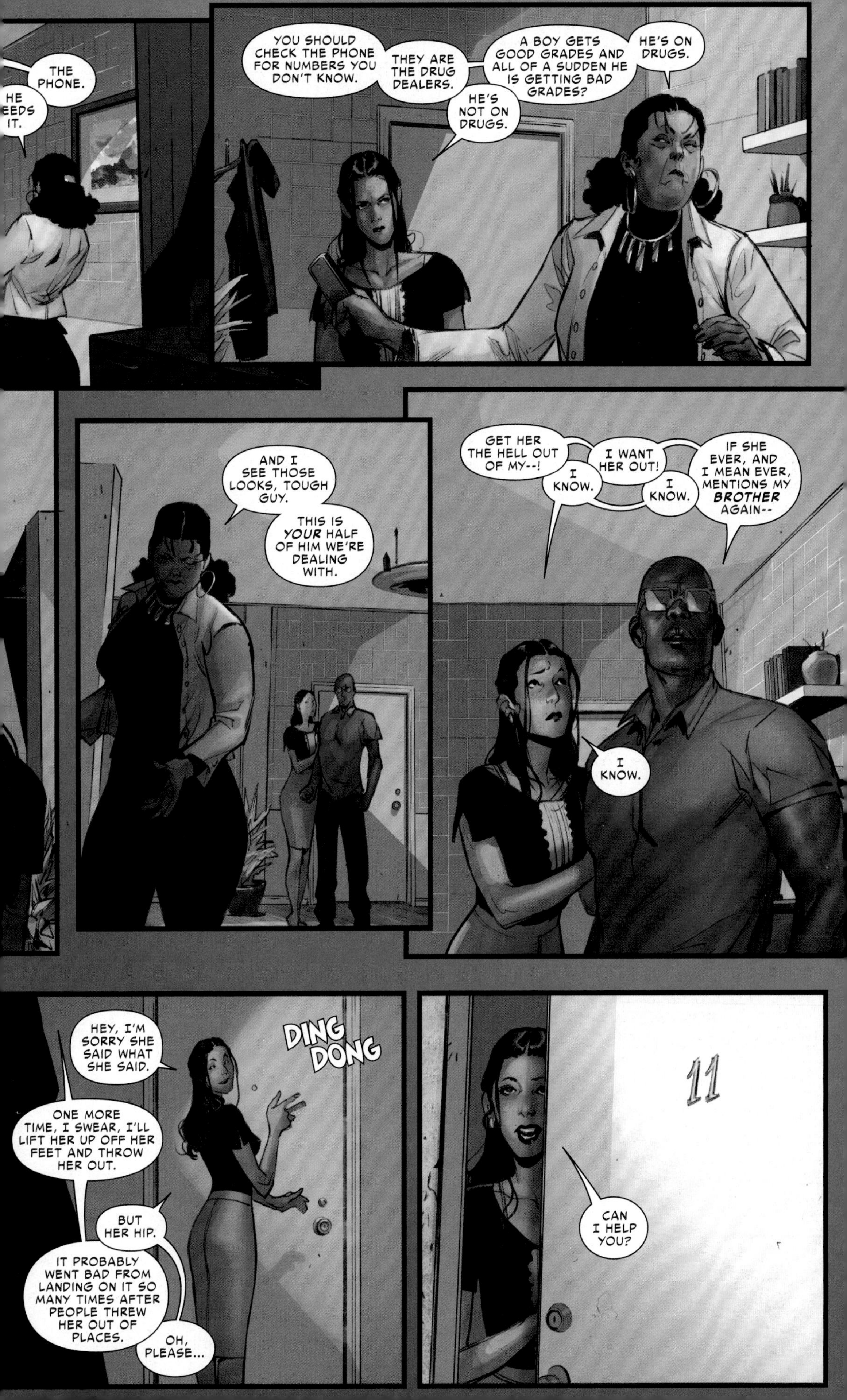

HE EEDS IT.
THE PHONE.
YOU SHOULD CHECK THE PHONE FOR NUMBERS YOU DON'T KNOW.
THEY ARE THE DRUG DEALERS.
HE'S NOT ON DRUGS.
A BOY GETS GOOD GRADES AND ALL OF A SUDDEN HE IS GETTING BAD GRADES?
HE'S ON DRUGS.
AND I SEE THOSE LOOKS, TOUGH GUY.
THIS IS *YOUR* HALF OF HIM WE'RE DEALING WITH.
GET HER THE HELL OUT OF MY--!
I KNOW.
I WANT HER OUT!
I KNOW.
IF SHE EVER, AND I MEAN EVER, MENTIONS MY ***BROTHER*** AGAIN--
I KNOW.
HEY, I'M SORRY SHE SAID WHAT SHE SAID.
DING DONG
ONE MORE TIME, I SWEAR, I'LL LIFT HER UP OFF HER FEET AND THROW HER OUT.
BUT HER HIP.
IT PROBABLY WENT BAD FROM LANDING ON IT SO MANY TIMES AFTER PEOPLE THREW HER OUT OF PLACES.
OH, PLEASE...
11
CAN I HELP YOU?

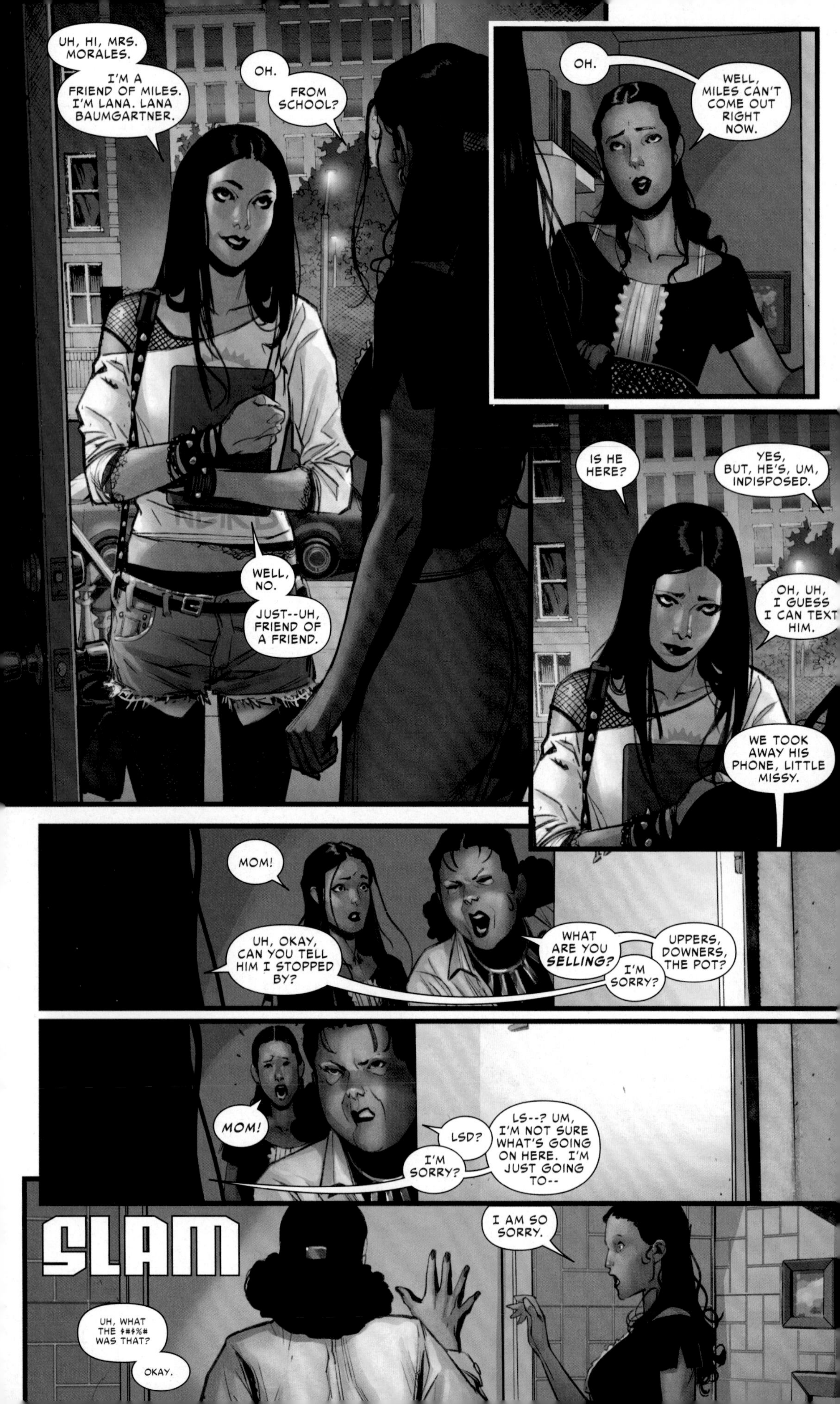
UH, HI, MRS. MORALES.
I'M A FRIEND OF MILES. I'M LANA. LANA BAUMGARTNER.
OH.
FROM SCHOOL?
WELL, NO.
JUST--UH, FRIEND OF A FRIEND.
OH.
WELL, MILES CAN'T COME OUT RIGHT NOW.
IS HE HERE?
YES, BUT, HE'S, UM, INDISPOSED.
OH, UH, I GUESS I CAN TEXT HIM.
WE TOOK AWAY HIS PHONE, LITTLE MISSY.
MOM!
UH, OKAY, CAN YOU TELL HIM I STOPPED BY?
WHAT ARE YOU SELLING?
I'M SORRY?
UPPERS, DOWNERS, THE POT?
MOM!
LSD?
I'M SORRY?
LS--? UM, I'M NOT SURE WHAT'S GOING ON HERE. I'M JUST GOING TO--
SLAM
I AM SO SORRY.
UH, WHAT THE $#¢%# WAS THAT?
OKAY.

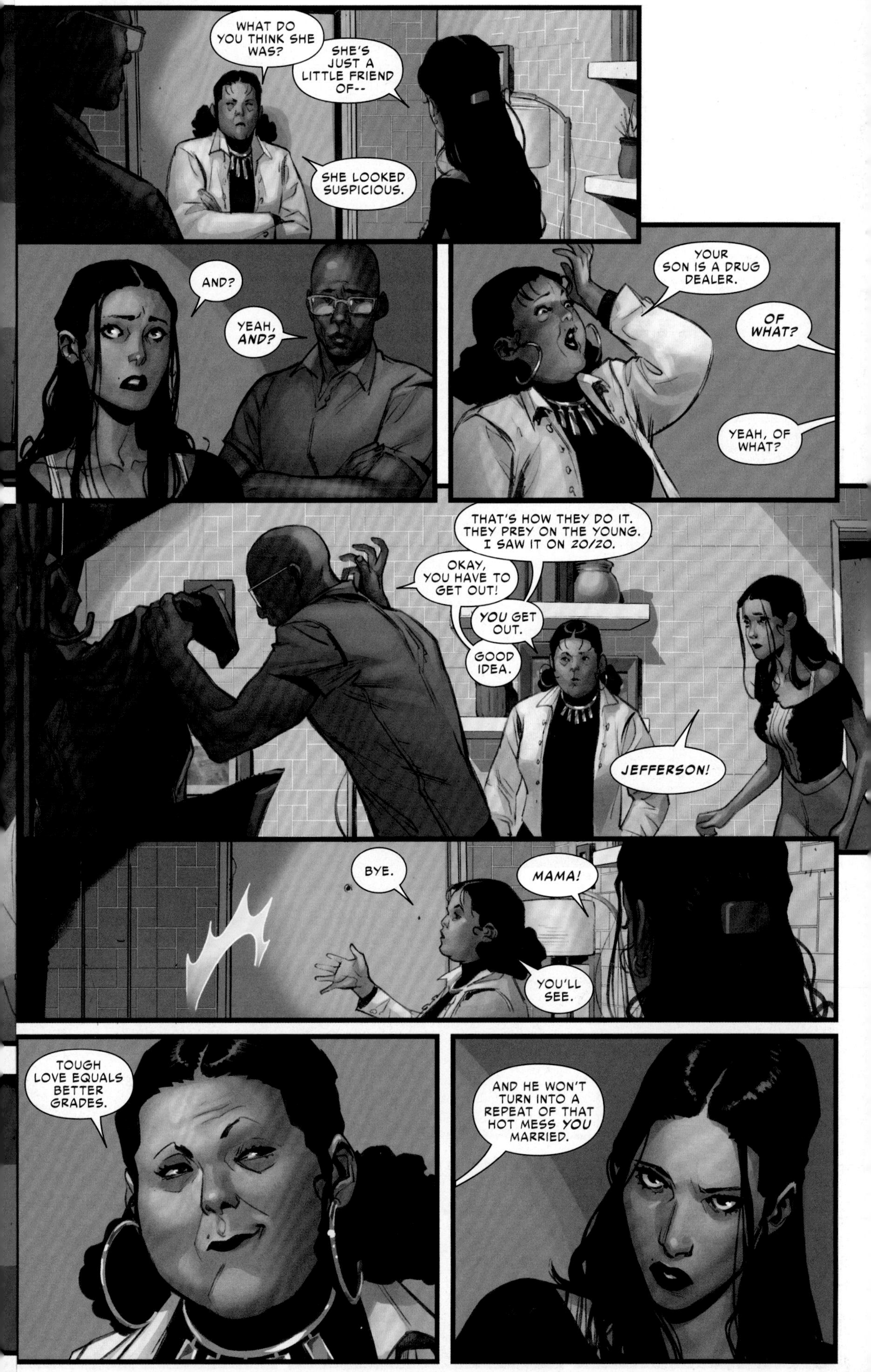
WHAT DO YOU THINK SHE WAS?
SHE'S JUST A LITTLE FRIEND OF--
SHE LOOKED SUSPICIOUS.
AND?
YEAH, AND?
YOUR SON IS A DRUG DEALER.
OF WHAT?
YEAH, OF WHAT?
THAT'S HOW THEY DO IT. THEY PREY ON THE YOUNG. I SAW IT ON 20/20.
OKAY, YOU HAVE TO GET OUT!
YOU GET OUT.
GOOD IDEA.
JEFFERSON!
BYE.
MAMA!
YOU'LL SEE.
TOUGH LOVE EQUALS BETTER GRADES.
AND HE WON'T TURN INTO A REPEAT OF THAT HOT MESS YOU MARRIED.

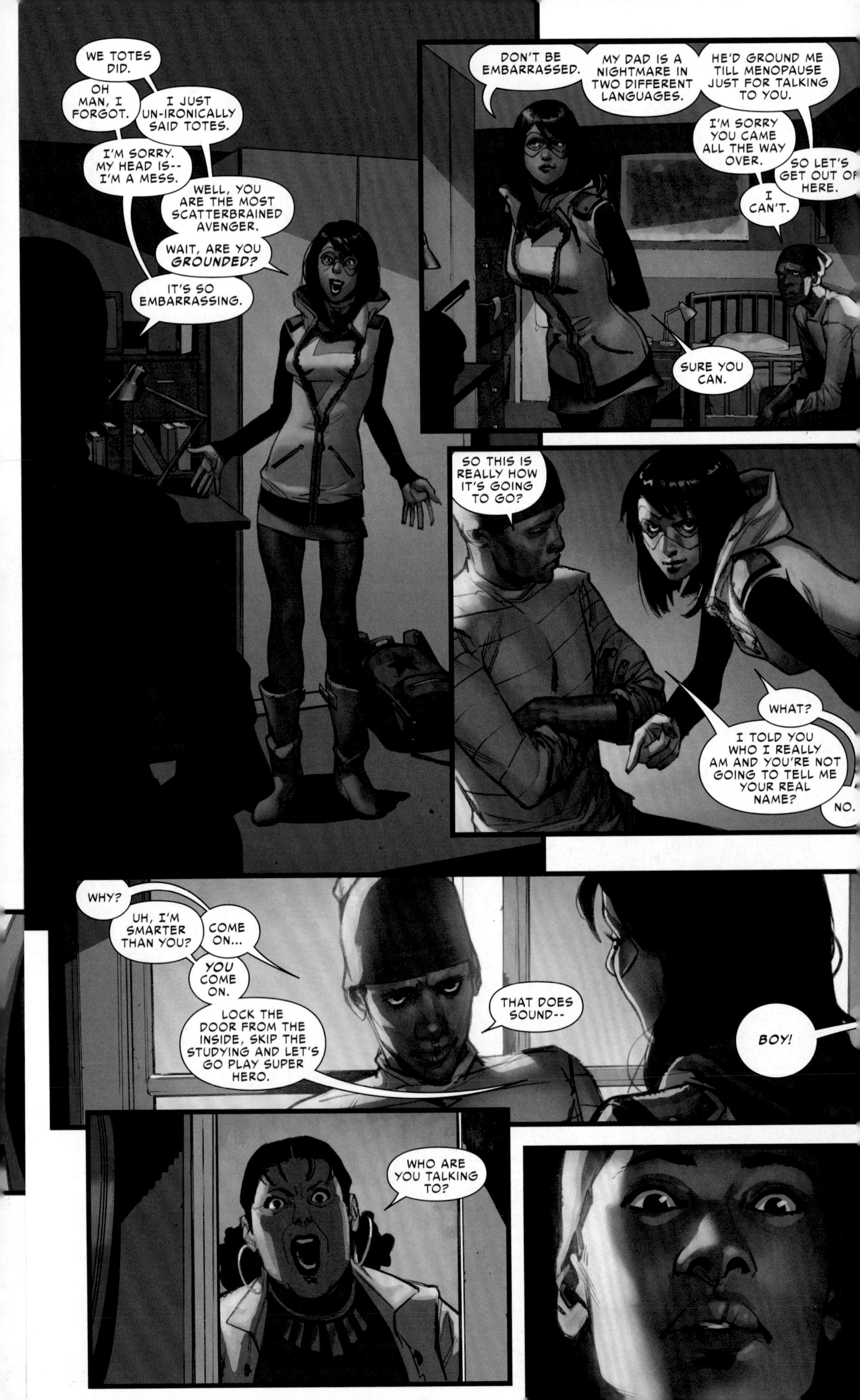
WE TOTES DID.
OH MAN, I FORGOT.
I JUST UN-IRONICALLY SAID TOTES.
I'M SORRY. MY HEAD IS-- I'M A MESS.
WELL, YOU ARE THE MOST SCATTERBRAINED AVENGER.
WAIT, ARE YOU *GROUNDED?*
IT'S SO EMBARRASSING.
DON'T BE EMBARRASSED.
MY DAD IS A NIGHTMARE IN TWO DIFFERENT LANGUAGES.
HE'D GROUND ME TILL MENOPAUSE JUST FOR TALKING TO YOU.
I'M SORRY YOU CAME ALL THE WAY OVER.
SO LET'S GET OUT OF HERE.
I CAN'T.
SURE YOU CAN.
SO THIS IS REALLY HOW IT'S GOING TO GO?
WHAT?
I TOLD YOU WHO I REALLY AM AND YOU'RE NOT GOING TO TELL ME YOUR REAL NAME?
NO.
WHY?
UH, I'M SMARTER THAN YOU?
COME ON...
YOU COME ON.
LOCK THE DOOR FROM THE INSIDE, SKIP THE STUDYING AND LET'S GO PLAY SUPER HERO.
THAT DOES SOUND--
BOY!
WHO ARE YOU TALKING TO?

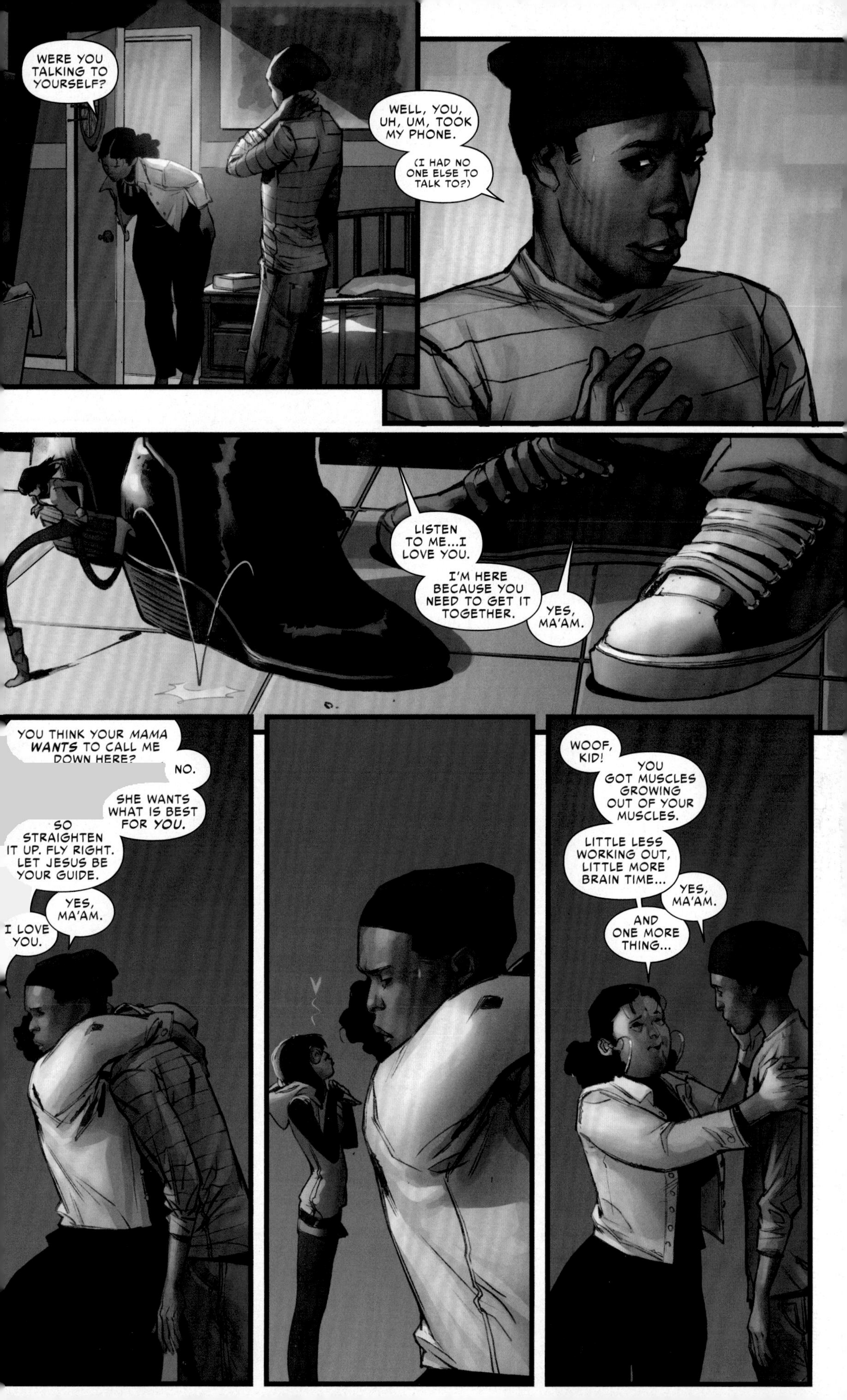
WERE YOU TALKING TO YOURSELF?
WELL, YOU, UH, UM, TOOK MY PHONE.
(I HAD NO ONE ELSE TO TALK TO?)
LISTEN TO ME...I LOVE YOU.
I'M HERE BECAUSE YOU NEED TO GET IT TOGETHER.
YES, MA'AM.
YOU THINK YOUR *MAMA* ***WANTS*** TO CALL ME DOWN HERE?
NO.
SHE WANTS WHAT IS BEST FOR ***YOU.***
SO STRAIGHTEN IT UP. FLY RIGHT. LET JESUS BE YOUR GUIDE.
YES, MA'AM.
I LOVE YOU.
WOOF, KID!
YOU GOT MUSCLES GROWING OUT OF YOUR MUSCLES.
LITTLE LESS WORKING OUT, LITTLE MORE BRAIN TIME...
YES, MA'AM.
AND ONE MORE THING...

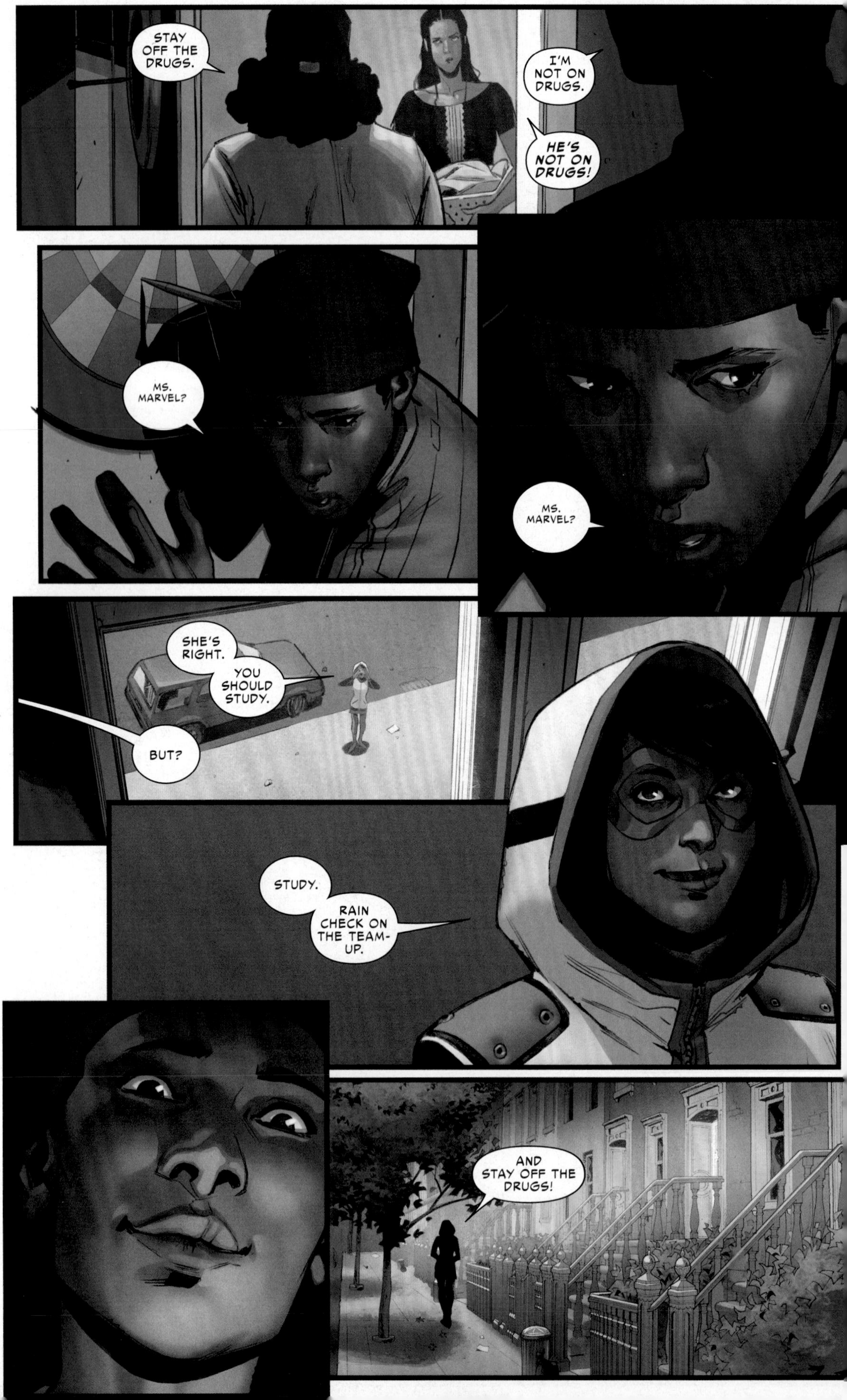
STAY OFF THE DRUGS.
I'M NOT ON DRUGS.
HE'S NOT ON DRUGS!
MS. MARVEL?
MS. MARVEL?
SHE'S RIGHT.
YOU SHOULD STUDY.
BUT?
STUDY.
RAIN CHECK ON THE TEAM-UP.
AND STAY OFF THE DRUGS!

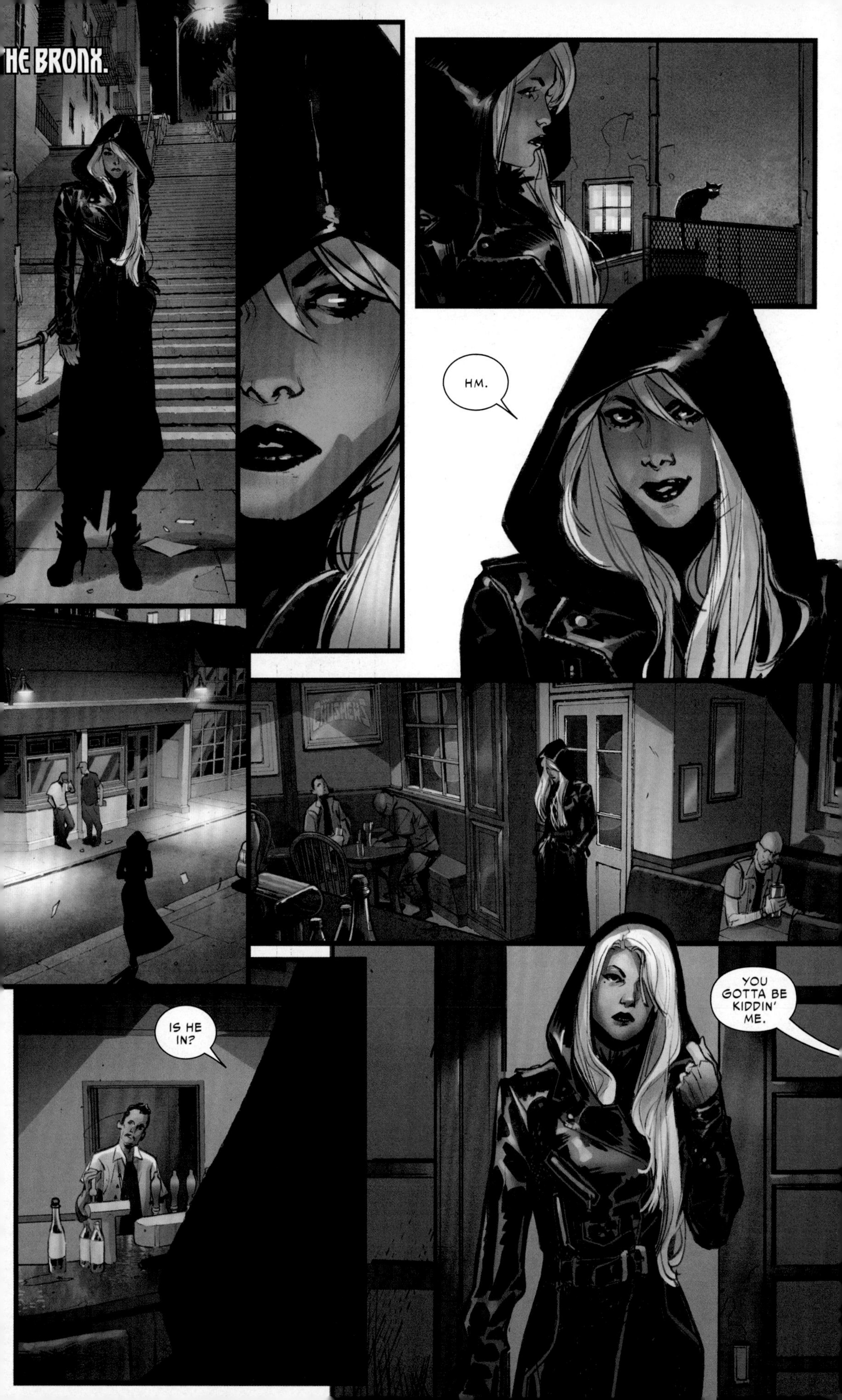

HE BRONX.
HM.
IS HE IN?
YOU GOTTA BE KIDDIN' ME.

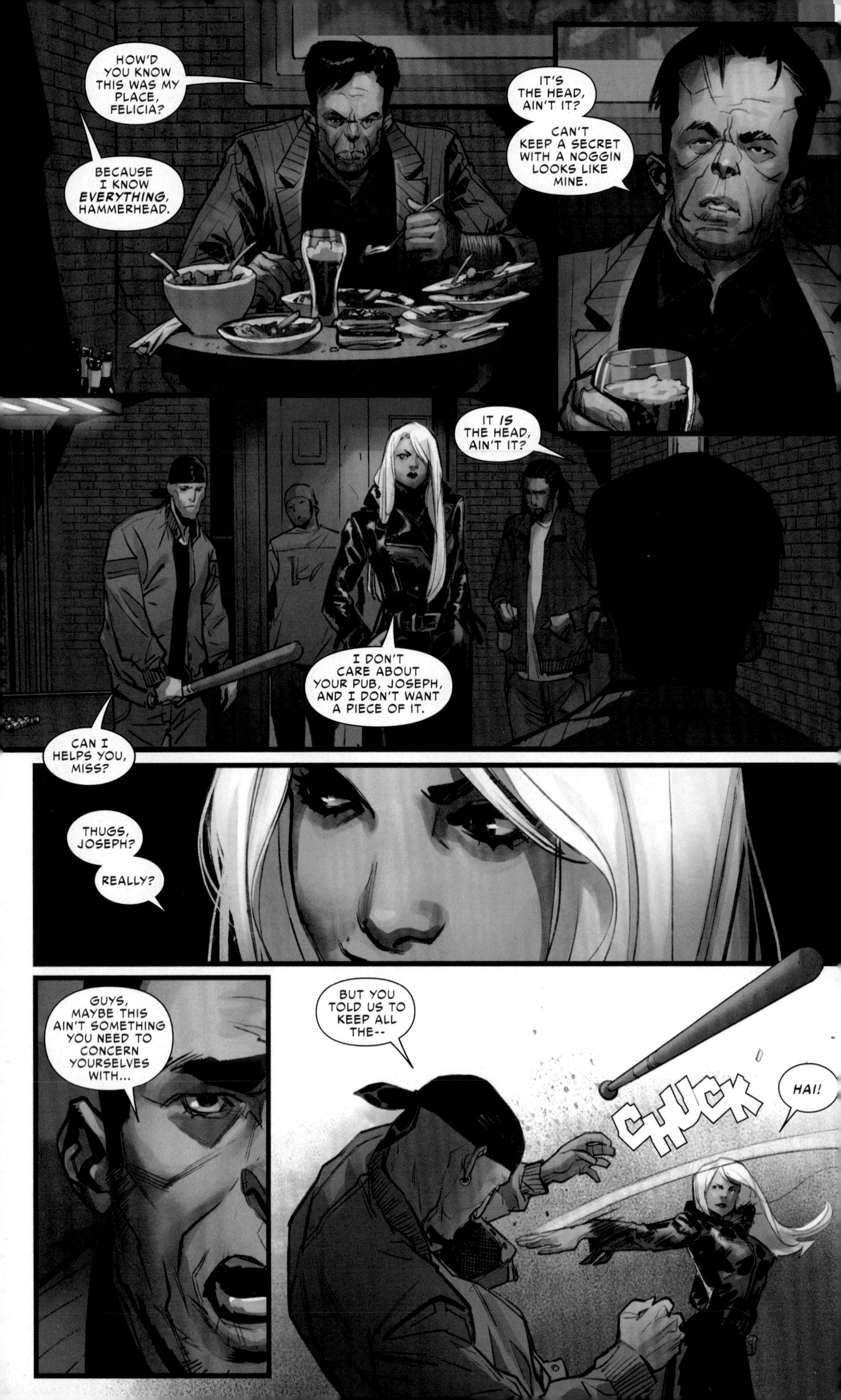
HOW'D YOU KNOW THIS WAS MY PLACE, FELICIA?
BECAUSE I KNOW *EVERYTHING*, HAMMERHEAD.
IT'S THE HEAD, AIN'T IT?
CAN'T KEEP A SECRET WITH A NOGGIN LOOKS LIKE MINE.
IT *IS* THE HEAD, AIN'T IT?
I DON'T CARE ABOUT YOUR PUB, JOSEPH, AND I DON'T WANT A PIECE OF IT.
CAN I HELPS YOU, MISS?
THUGS, JOSEPH?
REALLY?
GUYS, MAYBE THIS AIN'T SOMETHING YOU NEED TO CONCERN YOURSELVES WITH...
BUT YOU TOLD US TO KEEP ALL THE--
CHUCK
HAI!

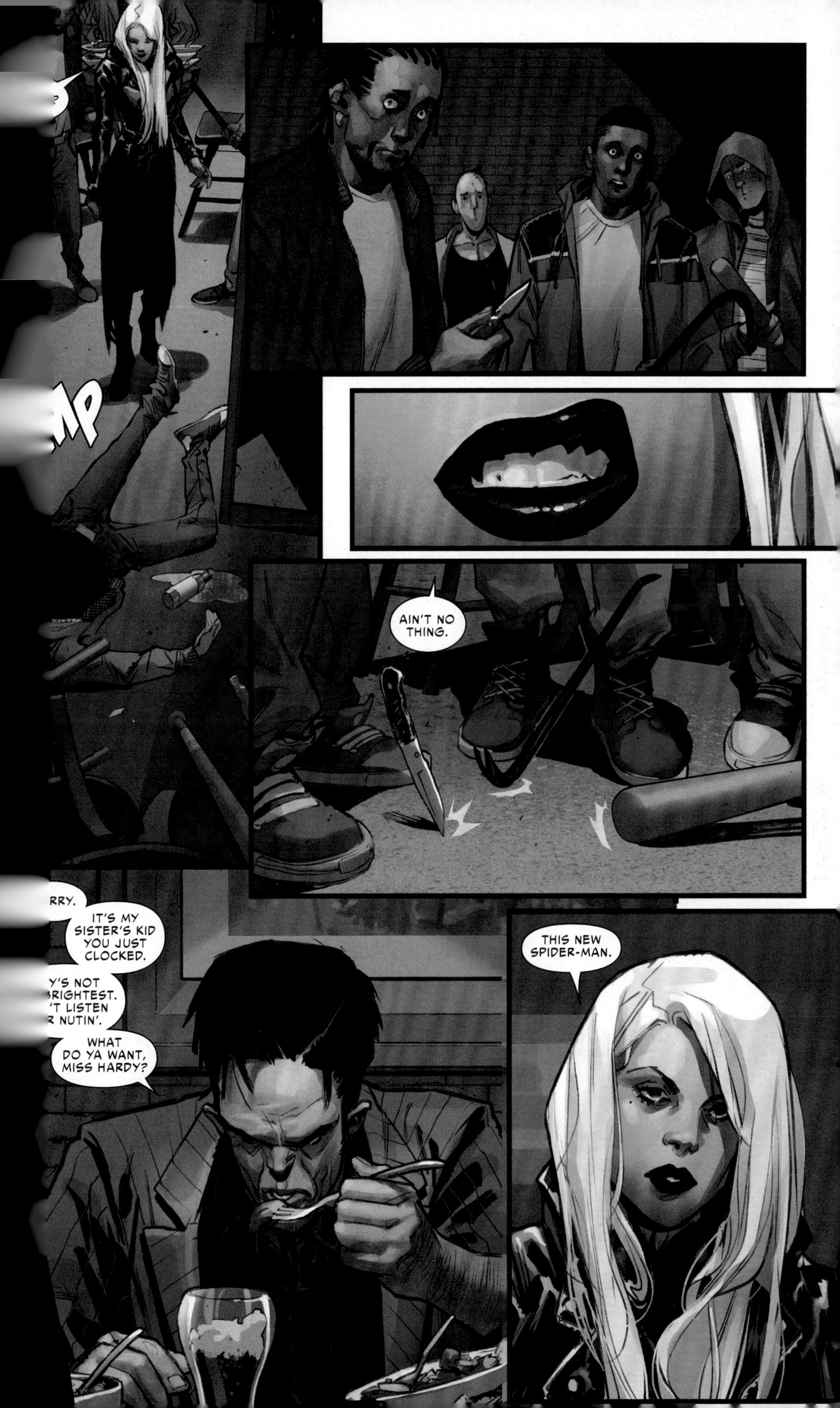

AIN'T NO THING.
RRY.
IT'S MY SISTER'S KID YOU JUST CLOCKED.
Y'S NOT BRIGHTEST. 'T LISTEN R NUTIN'.
WHAT DO YA WANT, MISS HARDY?
THIS NEW SPIDER-MAN.

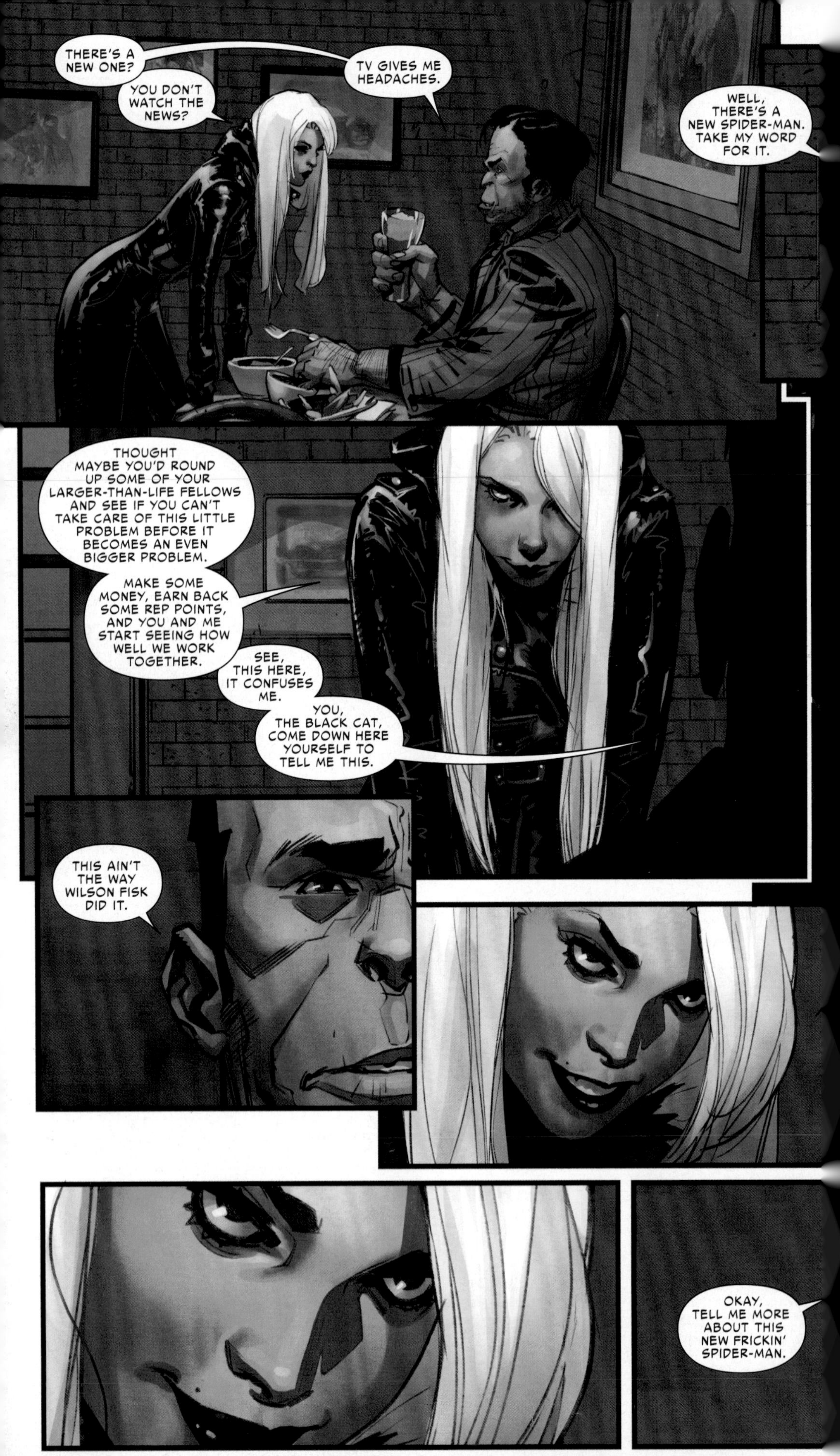
THERE'S A NEW ONE?
YOU DON'T WATCH THE NEWS?
TV GIVES ME HEADACHES.
WELL, THERE'S A NEW SPIDER-MAN. TAKE MY WORD FOR IT.
THOUGHT MAYBE YOU'D ROUND UP SOME OF YOUR LARGER-THAN-LIFE FELLOWS AND SEE IF YOU CAN'T TAKE CARE OF THIS LITTLE PROBLEM BEFORE IT BECOMES AN EVEN BIGGER PROBLEM.
MAKE SOME MONEY, EARN BACK SOME REP POINTS, AND YOU AND ME START SEEING HOW WELL WE WORK TOGETHER.
SEE, THIS HERE, IT CONFUSES ME.
YOU, THE BLACK CAT, COME DOWN HERE YOURSELF TO TELL ME THIS.
THIS AIN'T THE WAY WILSON FISK DID IT.
OKAY, TELL ME MORE ABOUT THIS NEW FRICKIN' SPIDER-MAN.

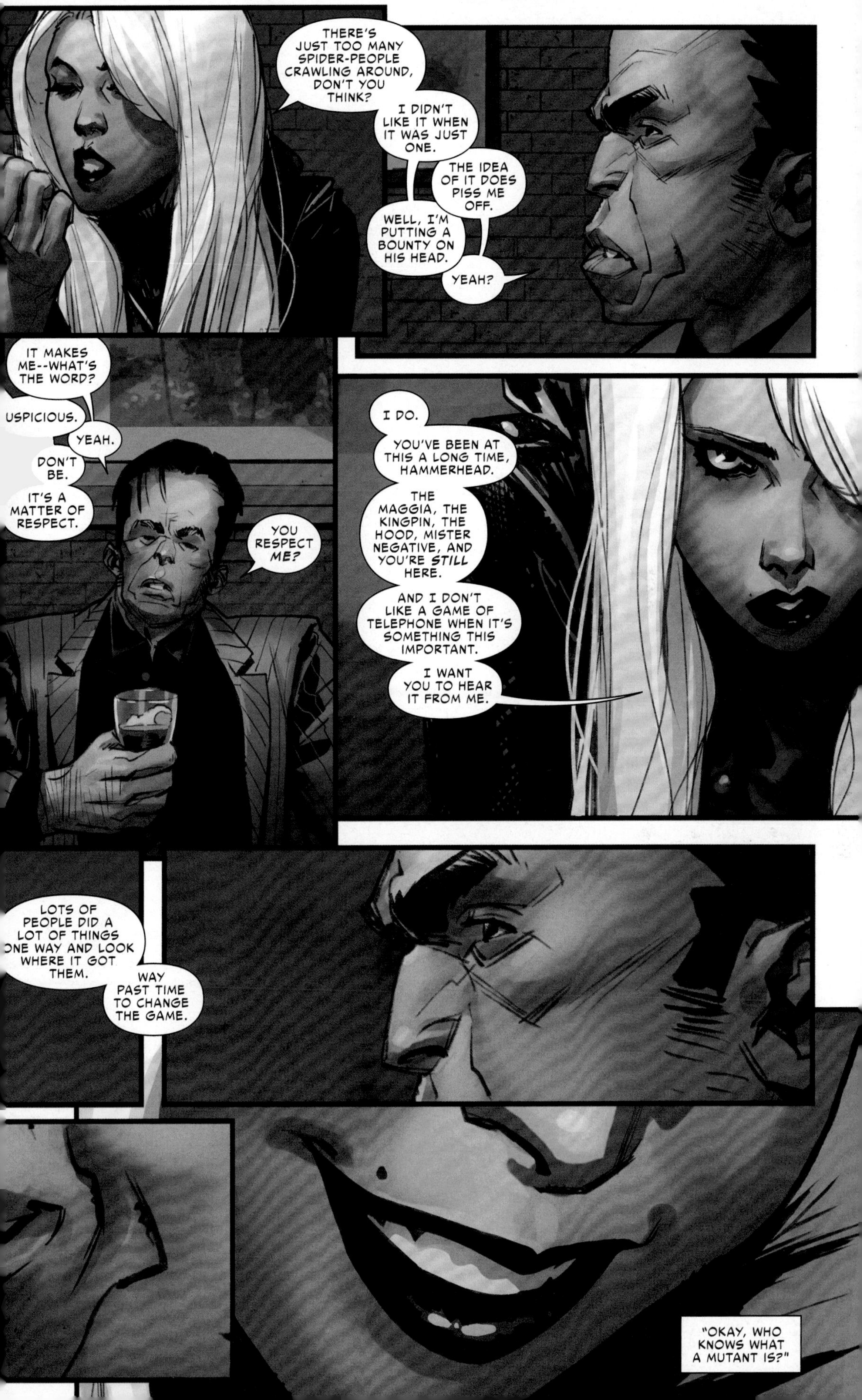

THERE'S JUST TOO MANY SPIDER-PEOPLE CRAWLING AROUND, DON'T YOU THINK?
I DIDN'T LIKE IT WHEN IT WAS JUST ONE.
THE IDEA OF IT DOES PISS ME OFF.
WELL, I'M PUTTING A BOUNTY ON HIS HEAD.
YEAH?
IT MAKES ME--WHAT'S THE WORD?
USPICIOUS.
YEAH.
DON'T BE.
IT'S A MATTER OF RESPECT.
YOU RESPECT *ME?*
I DO.
YOU'VE BEEN AT THIS A LONG TIME, HAMMERHEAD.
THE MAGGIA, THE KINGPIN, THE HOOD, MISTER NEGATIVE, AND YOU'RE *STILL* HERE.
AND I DON'T LIKE A GAME OF TELEPHONE WHEN IT'S SOMETHING THIS IMPORTANT.
I WANT YOU TO HEAR IT FROM ME.
LOTS OF PEOPLE DID A LOT OF THINGS ONE WAY AND LOOK WHERE IT GOT THEM.
WAY PAST TIME TO CHANGE THE GAME.
"OKAY, WHO KNOWS WHAT A MUTANT IS?"

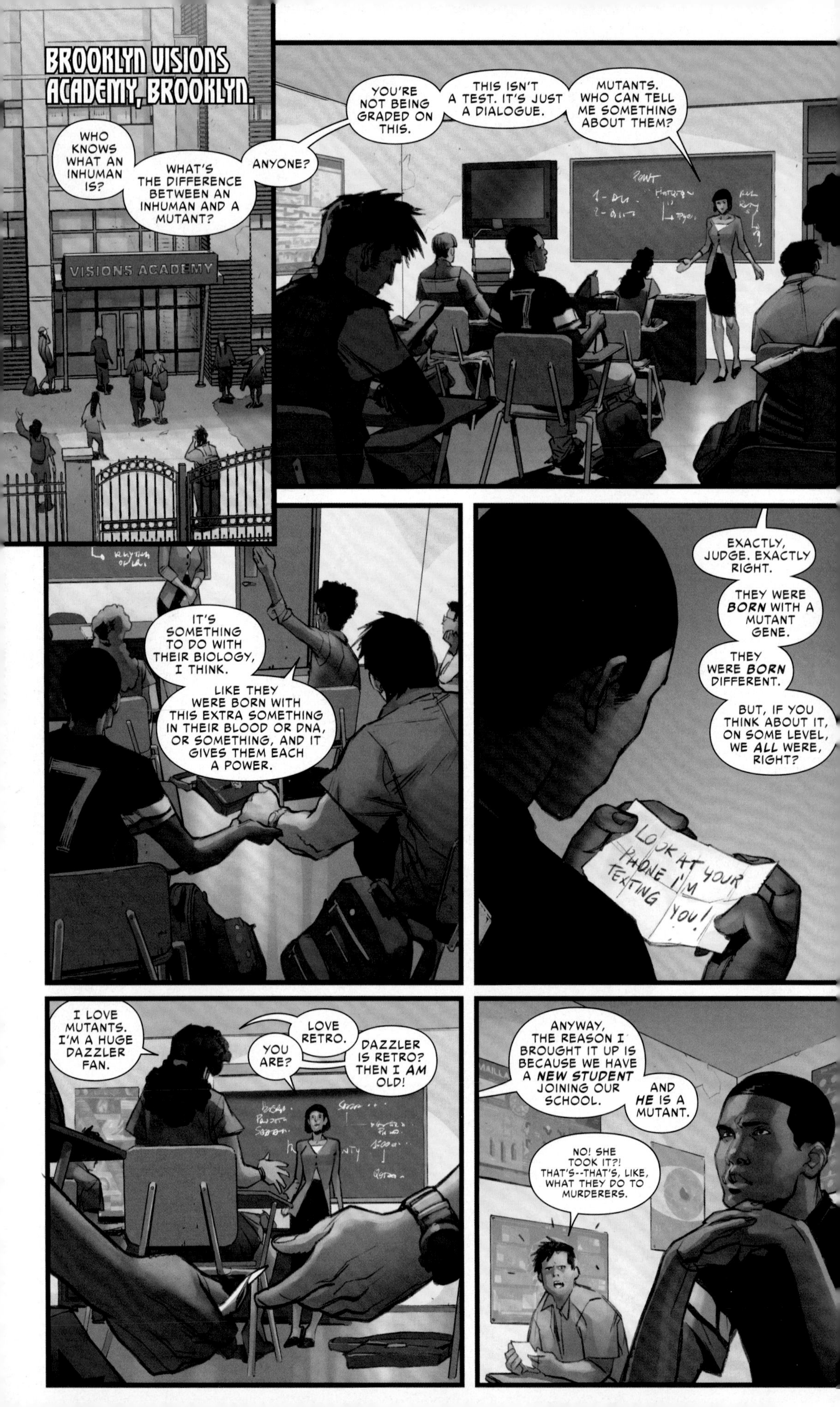
BROOKLYN VISIONS ACADEMY, BROOKLYN.
WHO KNOWS WHAT AN INHUMAN IS?
WHAT'S THE DIFFERENCE BETWEEN AN INHUMAN AND A MUTANT?
ANYONE?
VISIONS ACADEMY
YOU'RE NOT BEING GRADED ON THIS.
THIS ISN'T A TEST. IT'S JUST A DIALOGUE.
MUTANTS. WHO CAN TELL ME SOMETHING ABOUT THEM?
IT'S SOMETHING TO DO WITH THEIR BIOLOGY, I THINK.
LIKE THEY WERE BORN WITH THIS EXTRA SOMETHING IN THEIR BLOOD OR DNA, OR SOMETHING, AND IT GIVES THEM EACH A POWER.
EXACTLY, JUDGE. EXACTLY RIGHT.
THEY WERE BORN WITH A MUTANT GENE.
THEY WERE BORN DIFFERENT.
BUT, IF YOU THINK ABOUT IT, ON SOME LEVEL, WE ALL WERE, RIGHT?
LOOK AT YOUR PHONE I'M TEXTING YOU!
I LOVE MUTANTS. I'M A HUGE DAZZLER FAN.
YOU ARE?
LOVE RETRO.
DAZZLER IS RETRO? THEN I AM OLD!
ANYWAY, THE REASON I BROUGHT IT UP IS BECAUSE WE HAVE A NEW STUDENT JOINING OUR SCHOOL.
AND HE IS A MUTANT.
NO! SHE TOOK IT?! THAT'S--THAT'S, LIKE, WHAT THEY DO TO MURDERERS.

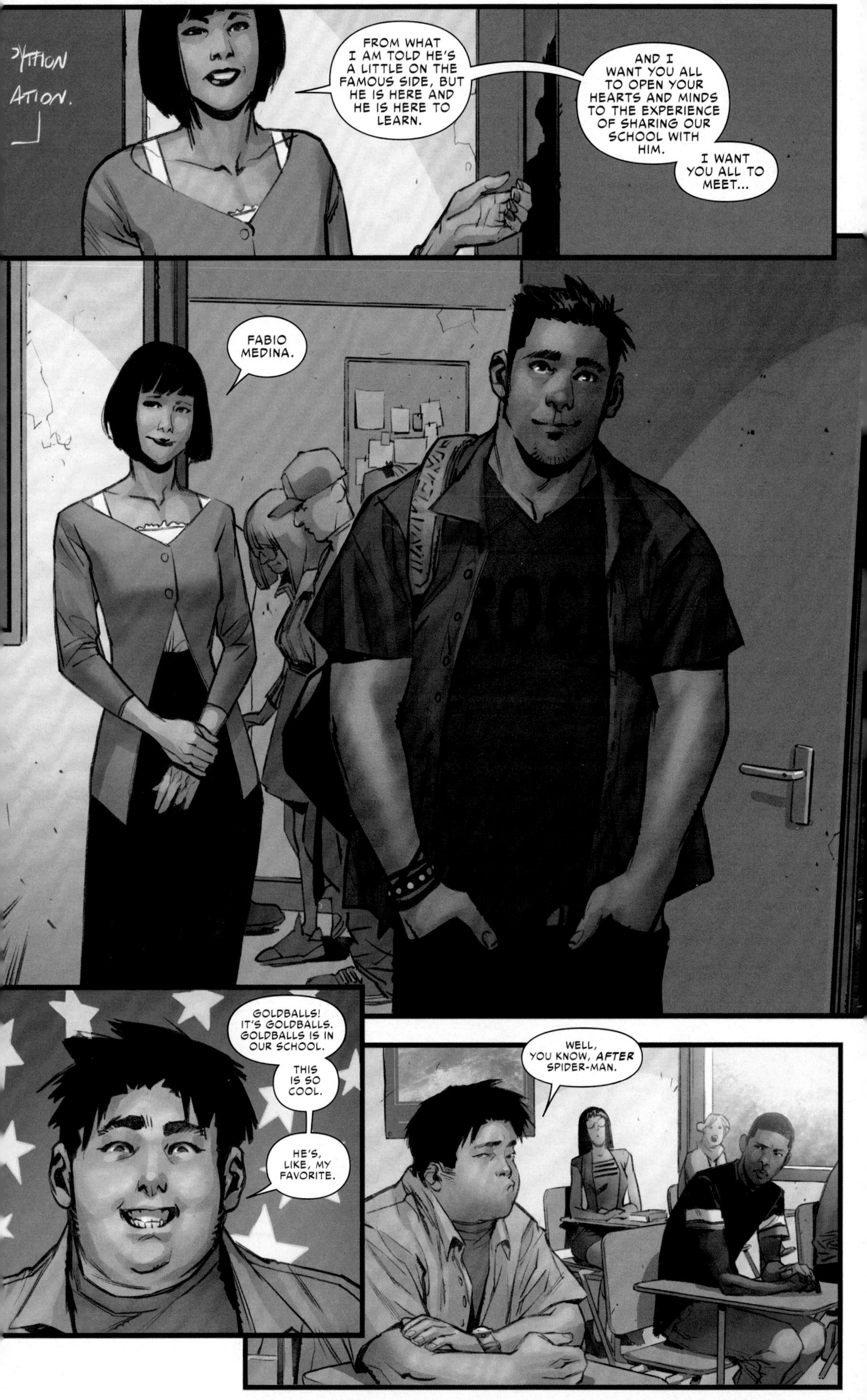
FROM WHAT I AM TOLD HE'S A LITTLE ON THE FAMOUS SIDE, BUT HE IS HERE AND HE IS HERE TO LEARN.
AND I WANT YOU ALL TO OPEN YOUR HEARTS AND MINDS TO THE EXPERIENCE OF SHARING OUR SCHOOL WITH HIM.
I WANT YOU ALL TO MEET...
FABIO MEDINA.
GOLDBALLS! IT'S GOLDBALLS. GOLDBALLS IS IN OUR SCHOOL.
THIS IS SO COOL.
HE'S, LIKE, MY FAVORITE.
WELL, YOU KNOW, *AFTER* SPIDER-MAN.

KHARY RANDOLPH & EMILIO LOPEZ
2 VARIANT

PASCAL CAMPION
3 VARIANT

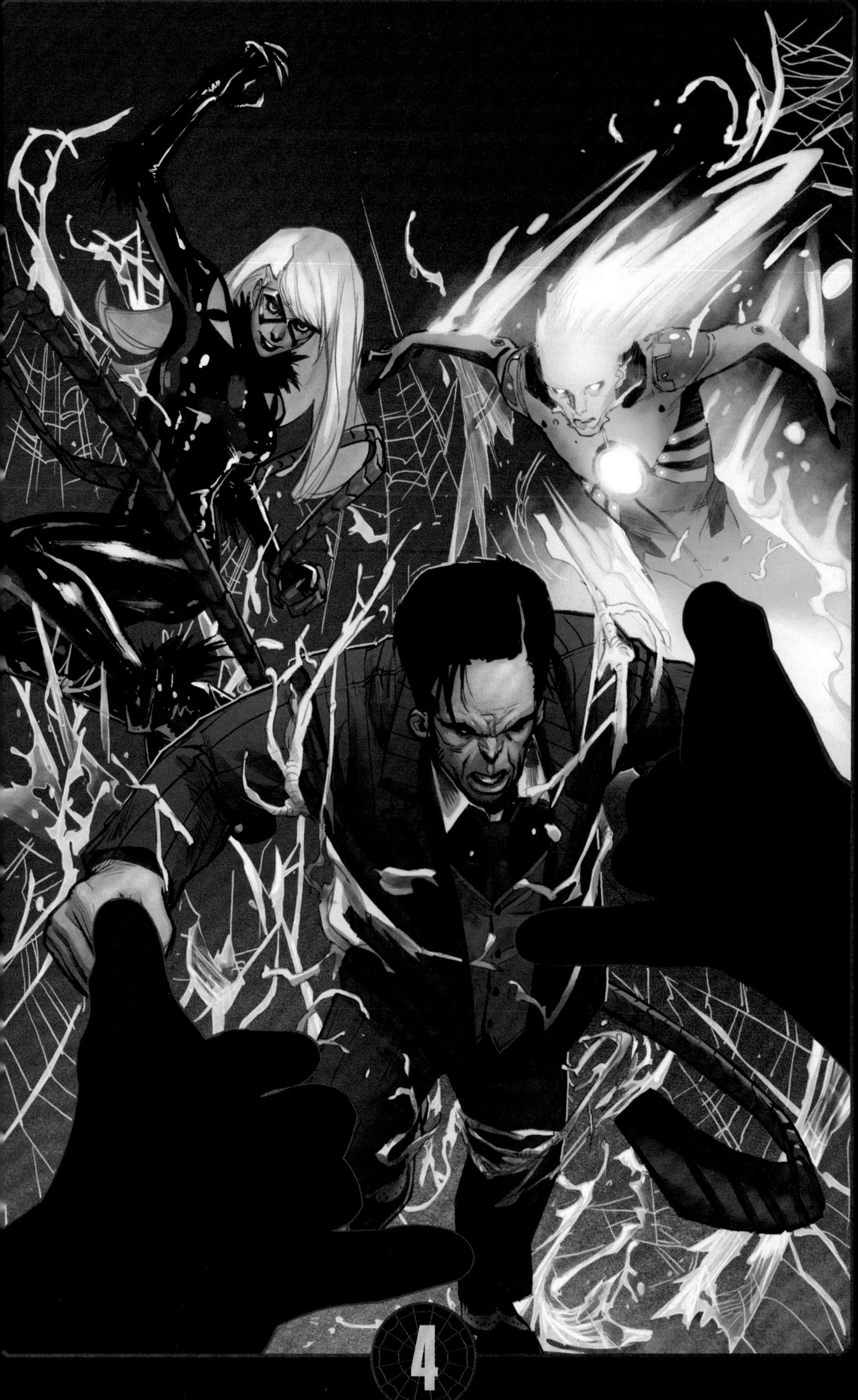
4

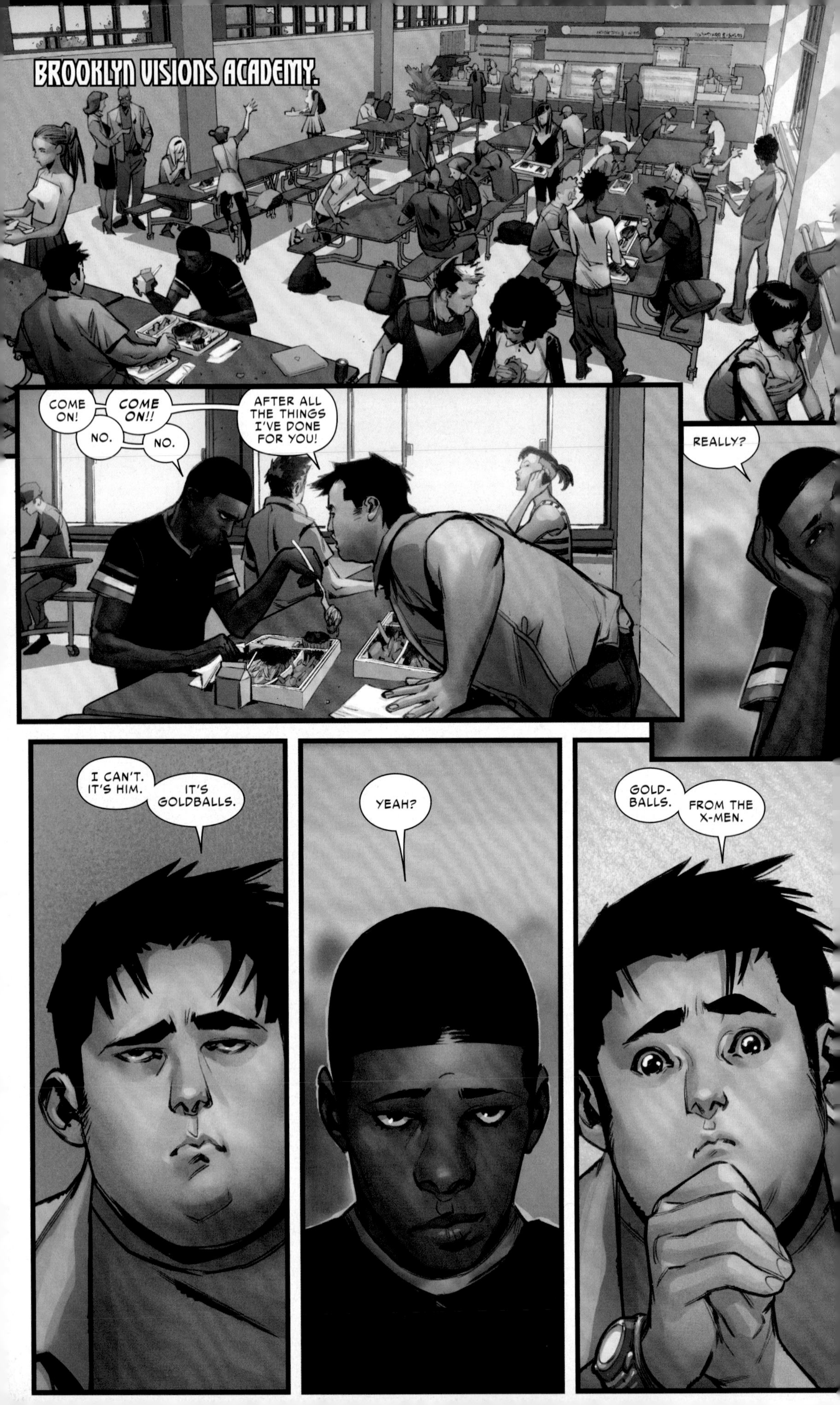
BROOKLYN VISIONS ACADEMY.
COME ON!
NO.
COME ON!!
NO.
AFTER ALL THE THINGS I'VE DONE FOR YOU!
REALLY?
I CAN'T. IT'S HIM.
IT'S GOLDBALLS.
YEAH?
GOLD-BALLS.
FROM THE X-MEN.

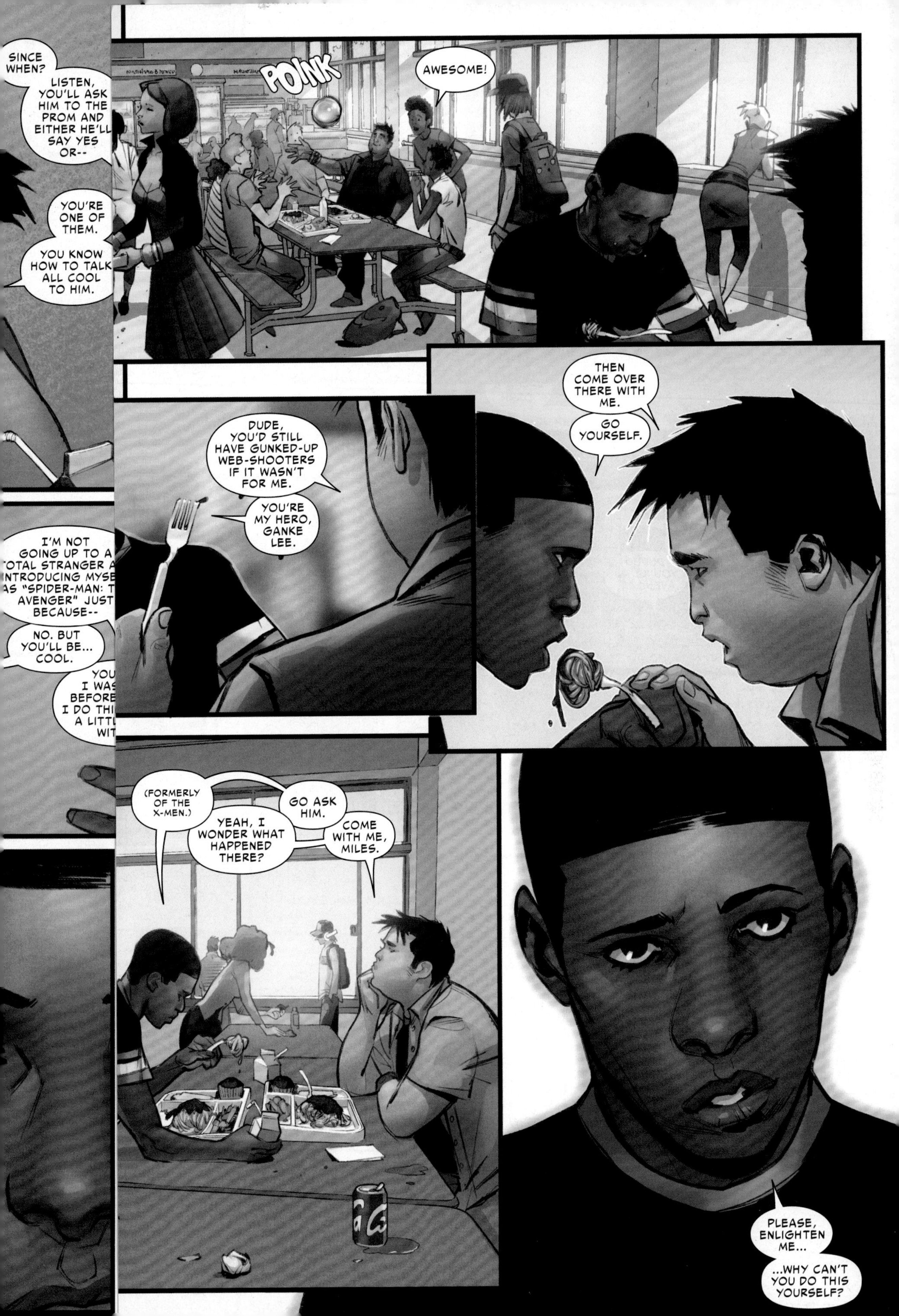
SINCE WHEN?
LISTEN, YOU'LL ASK HIM TO THE PROM AND EITHER HE'LL SAY YES OR--
YOU'RE ONE OF THEM.
YOU KNOW HOW TO TALK ALL COOL TO HIM.
I'M NOT GOING UP TO A TOTAL STRANGER A INTRODUCING MYSE AS "SPIDER-MAN: T AVENGER" JUST BECAUSE--
NO. BUT YOU'LL BE... COOL.
POINK
AWESOME!
DUDE, YOU'D STILL HAVE GUNKED-UP WEB-SHOOTERS IF IT WASN'T FOR ME.
YOU'RE MY HERO, GANKE LEE.
THEN COME OVER THERE WITH ME.
GO YOURSELF.
GO ASK HIM.
(FORMERLY OF THE X-MEN.)
YEAH, I WONDER WHAT HAPPENED THERE?
COME WITH ME, MILES.
PLEASE, ENLIGHTEN ME...
...WHY CAN'T YOU DO THIS YOURSELF?

WHERE DOES IT COME FROM?

WHERE DOES IT GO?

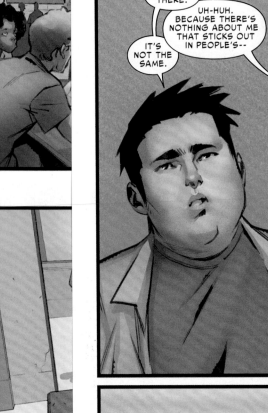

YOU DON'T KNOW WHAT IT FEELS LIKE TO BE-- TO BE BIGGER THAN YOU WANT TO BE.

YEAH?

IT'S HARD OUT THERE.

UH-HUH. BECAUSE THERE'S NOTHING ABOUT ME THAT STICKS OUT IN PEOPLE'S--

IT'S NOT THE SAME.

YEAH? TRY WALKING INTO A DUANE READE AND HAVE AN ITCHY SECURITY GUARD JUST FOLLOW YOU AROUND JUST BECAUSE...

WHEN I WAS NINE YEARS OLD, I SAW AN OLD WOMAN CROSS THE STREET TO AVOID WALKING BY ME.

NINE YEARS OLD.

OKAY, SO YOU'RE BLACK.

BIG WHUP.

AND HISPANIC.

WE LIVE IN NEW YORK.

NO ONE CARES WHAT COLOR YOU ARE ANYMORE--

AND THERE'S NO CHUBBY PEOPLE IN THE FIVE BOROUGHS?

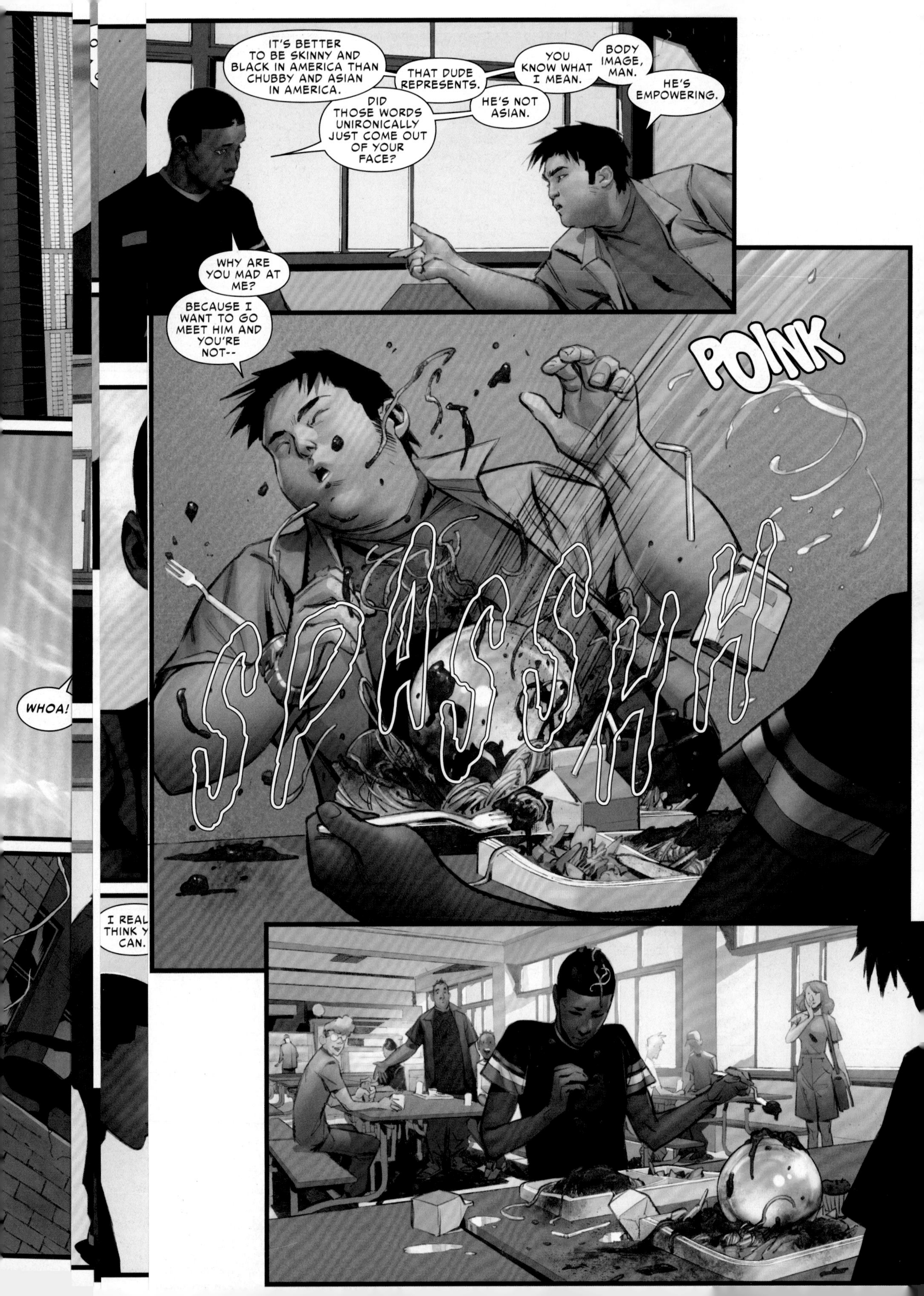
IT'S BETTER TO BE SKINNY AND BLACK IN AMERICA THAN CHUBBY AND ASIAN IN AMERICA.
THAT DUDE REPRESENTS.
YOU KNOW WHAT I MEAN.
BODY IMAGE, MAN.
HE'S EMPOWERING.
DID THOSE WORDS UNIRONICALLY JUST COME OUT OF YOUR FACE?
HE'S NOT ASIAN.
WHY ARE YOU MAD AT ME?
BECAUSE I WANT TO GO MEET HIM AND YOU'RE NOT--
POINK
SPASSHH
WHOA!

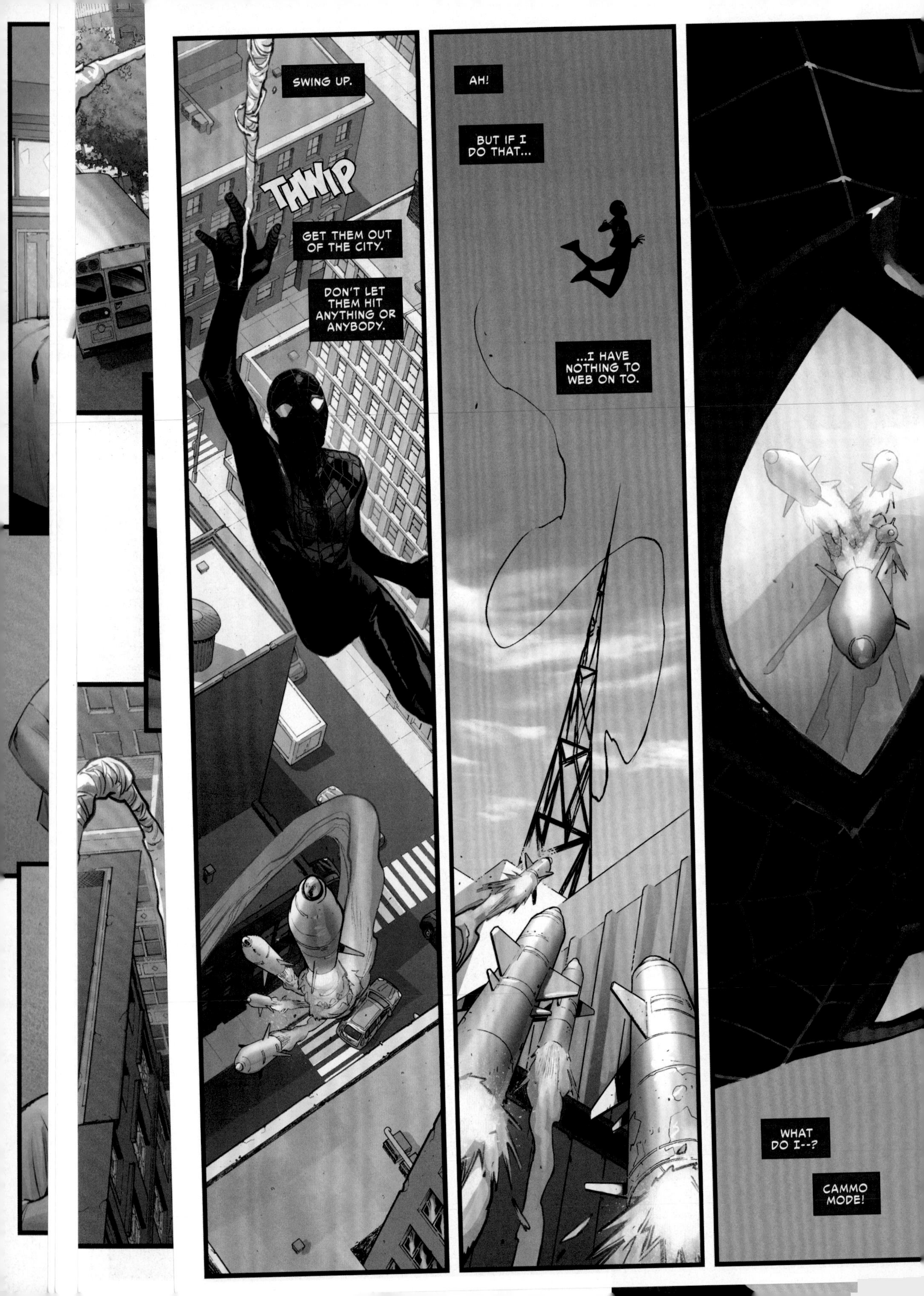
SWING UP.
THWIP
GET THEM OUT OF THE CITY.
DON'T LET THEM HIT ANYTHING OR ANYBODY.
AH!
BUT IF I DO THAT...
...I HAVE NOTHING TO WEB ON TO.
WHAT DO I--?
CAMMO MODE!

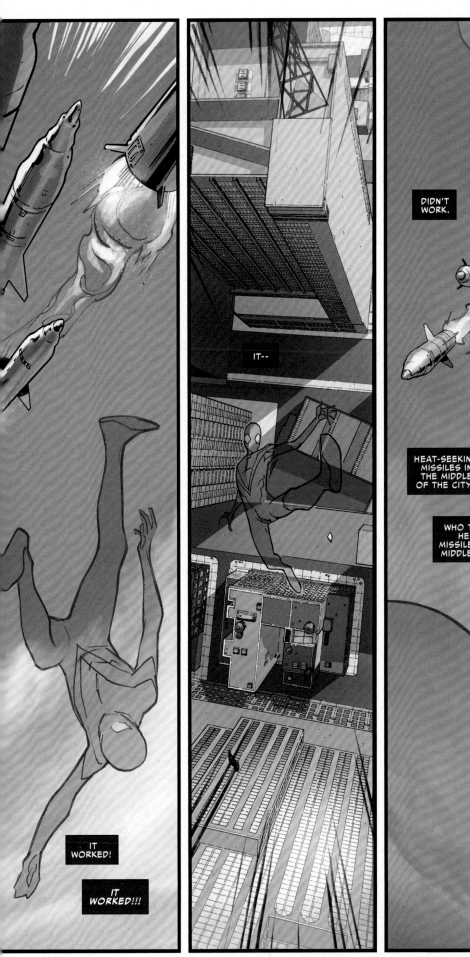

IT
WORKED!

IT
WORKED!!!

IT--

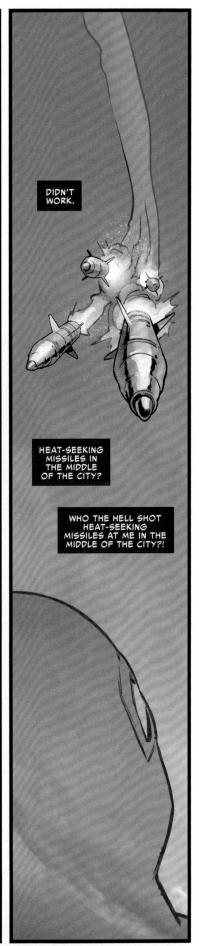

DIDN'T
WORK.

HEAT-SEEKING
MISSILES IN
THE MIDDLE
OF THE CITY?

WHO THE HELL SHOT
HEAT-SEEKING
MISSILES AT ME IN THE
MIDDLE OF THE CITY?!

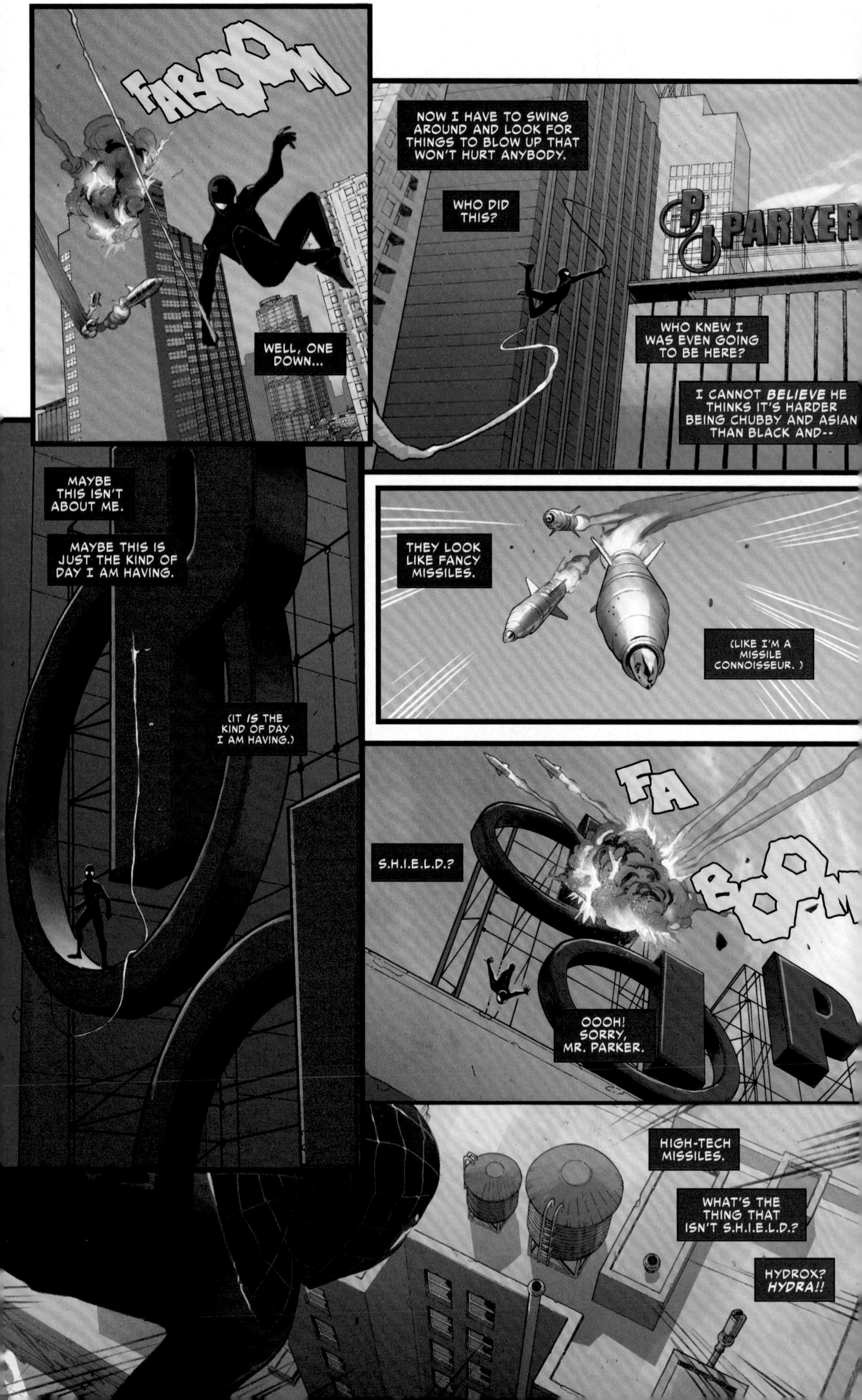
FABOOM
WELL, ONE DOWN...
NOW I HAVE TO SWING AROUND AND LOOK FOR THINGS TO BLOW UP THAT WON'T HURT ANYBODY.
WHO DID THIS?
PI PARKER
WHO KNEW I WAS EVEN GOING TO BE HERE?
I CANNOT *BELIEVE* HE THINKS IT'S HARDER BEING CHUBBY AND ASIAN THAN BLACK AND--
MAYBE THIS ISN'T ABOUT ME.
MAYBE THIS IS JUST THE KIND OF DAY I AM HAVING.
(IT *IS* THE KIND OF DAY I AM HAVING.)
THEY LOOK LIKE FANCY MISSILES.
(LIKE I'M A MISSILE CONNOISSEUR.)
FA BOOM
S.H.I.E.L.D.?
OOOH! SORRY, MR. PARKER.
HIGH-TECH MISSILES.
WHAT'S THE THING THAT ISN'T S.H.I.E.L.D.?
HYDROX? *HYDRA!!*

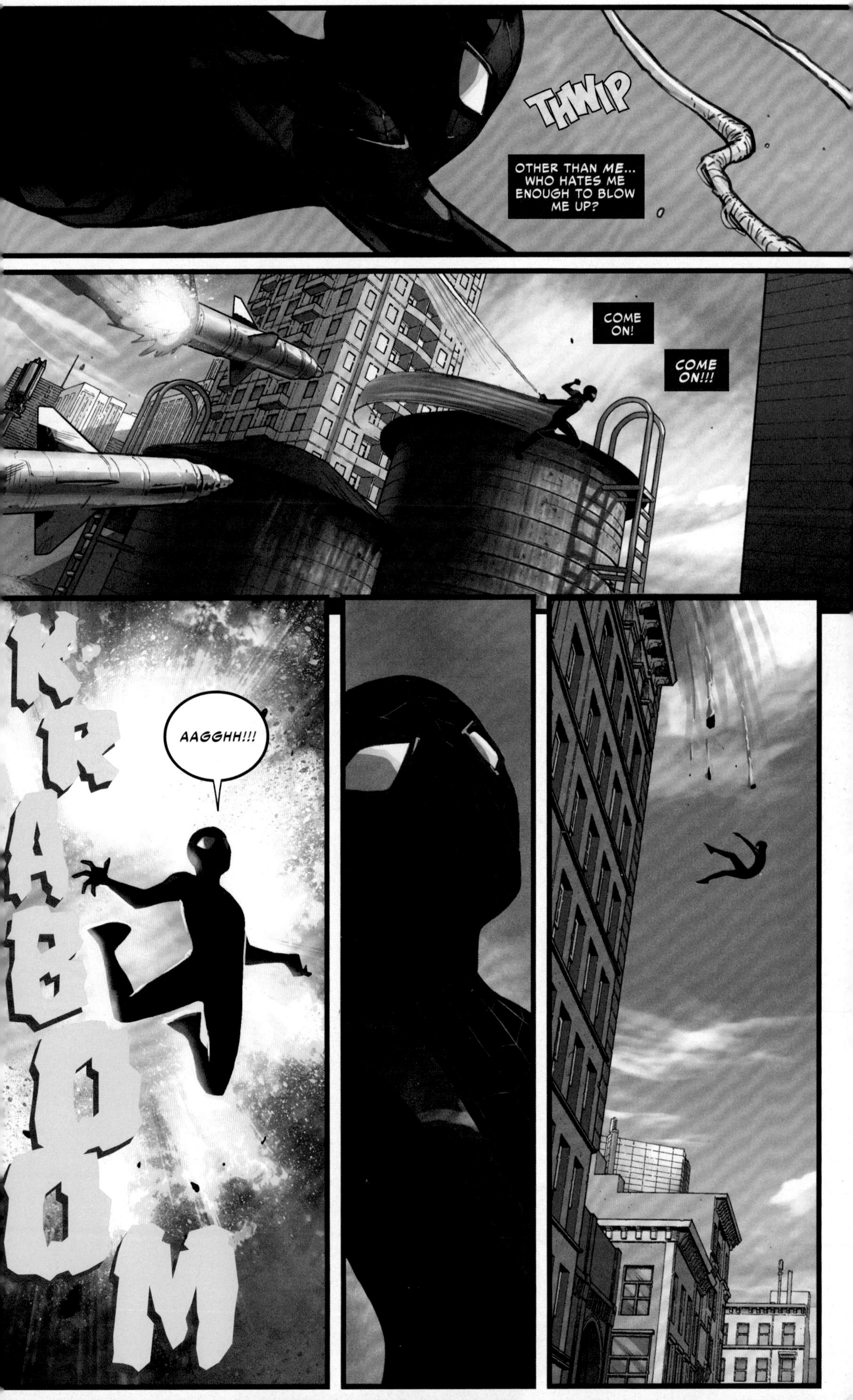
THWIP
OTHER THAN *ME*... WHO HATES ME ENOUGH TO BLOW ME UP?
COME ON!
COME ON!!!
KRABOOM
AAGGHH!!!

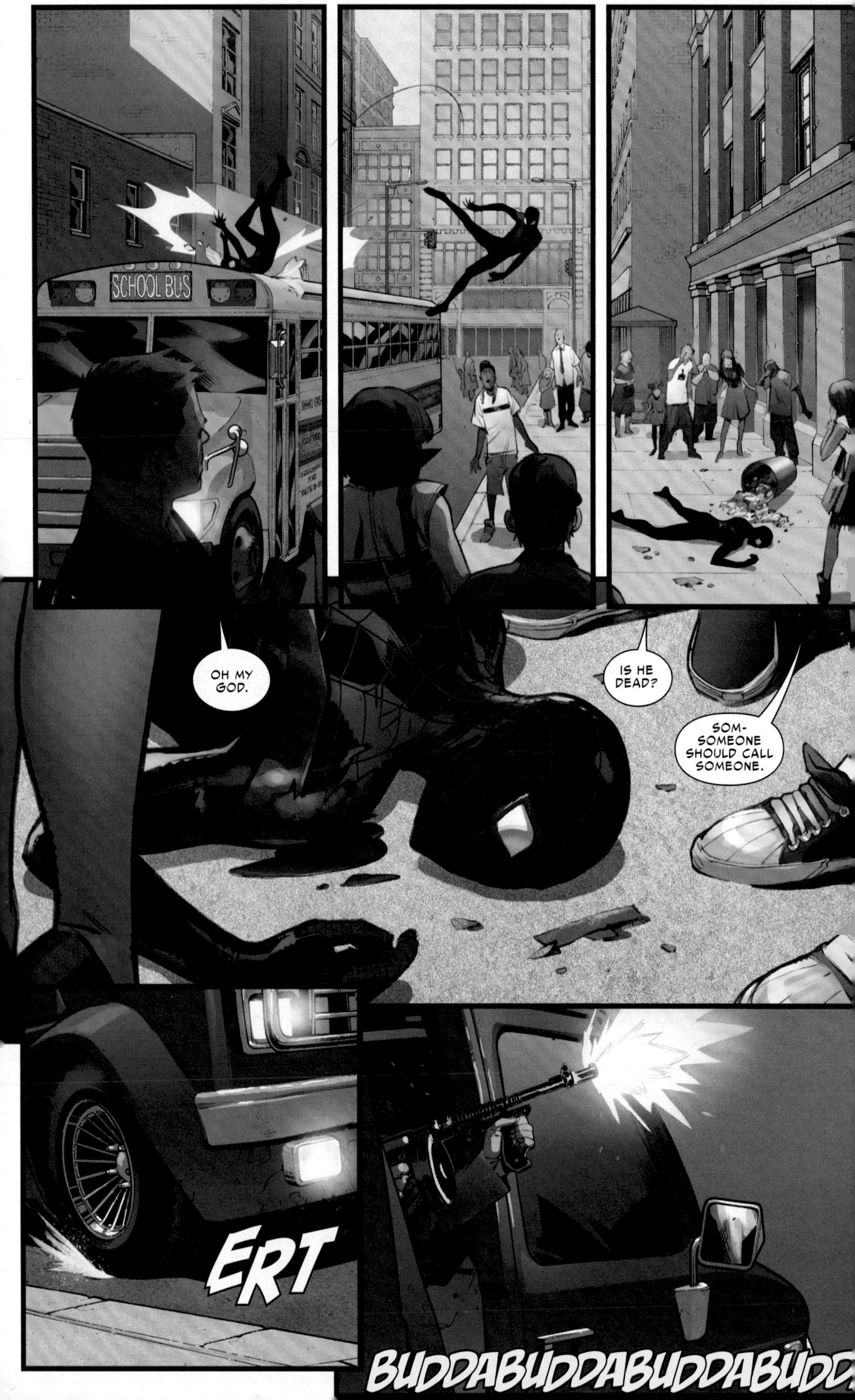
SCHOOL BUS
OH MY GOD.
IS HE DEAD?
SOM- SOMEONE SHOULD CALL SOMEONE.
ERT
BUDDABUDDABUDDABUDD

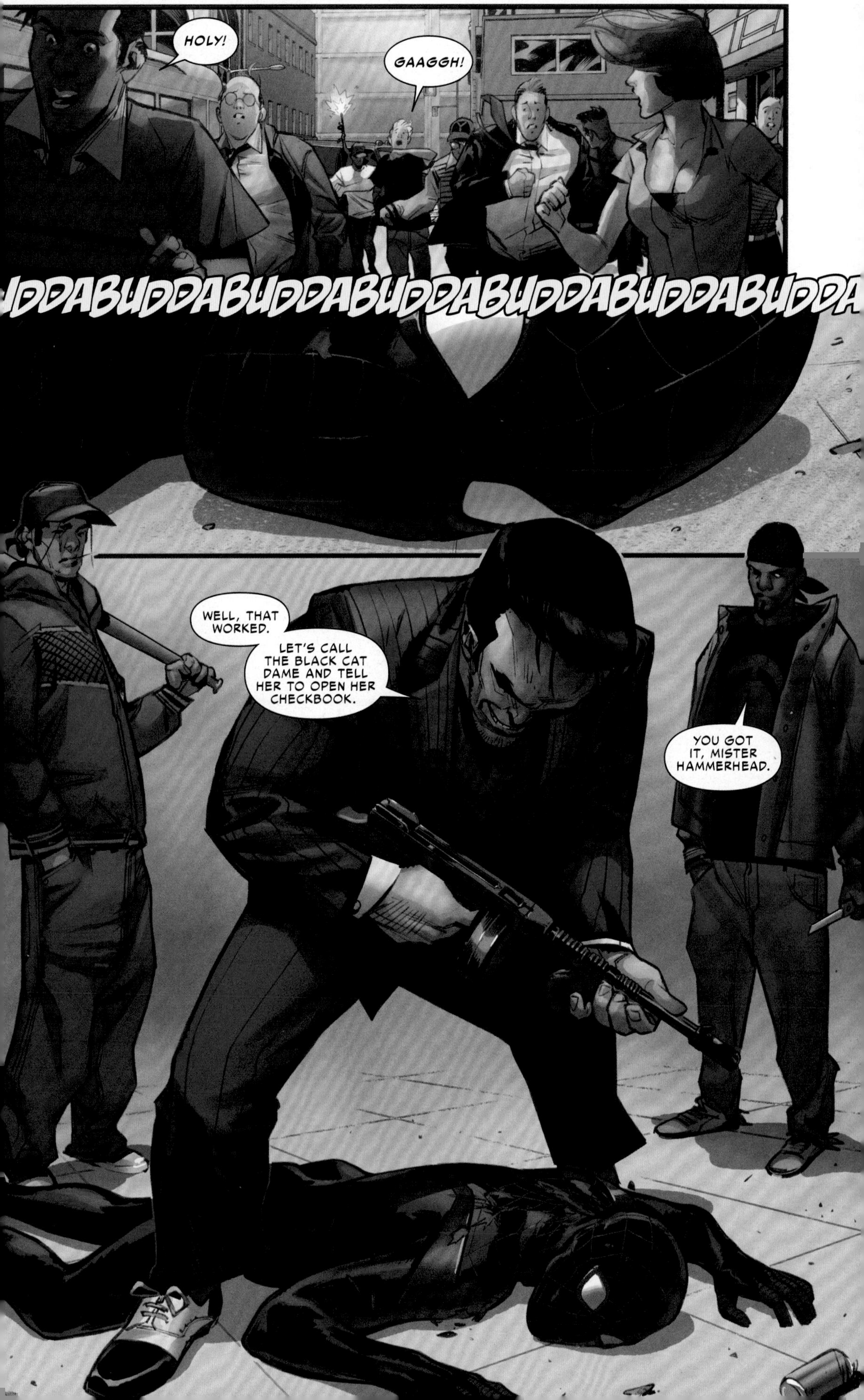
HOLY!
GAAGGH!
IDDABUDDABUDDABUDDABUDDABUDDABUDDA
WELL, THAT WORKED.
LET'S CALL THE BLACK CAT DAME AND TELL HER TO OPEN HER CHECKBOOK.
YOU GOT IT, MISTER HAMMERHEAD.

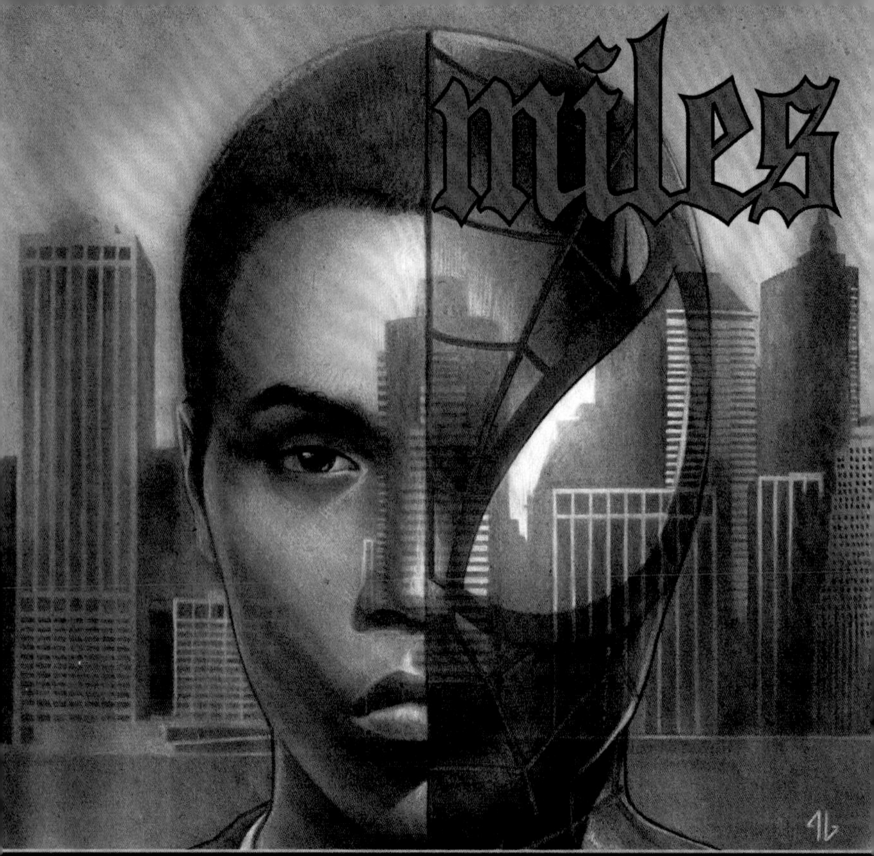
miles

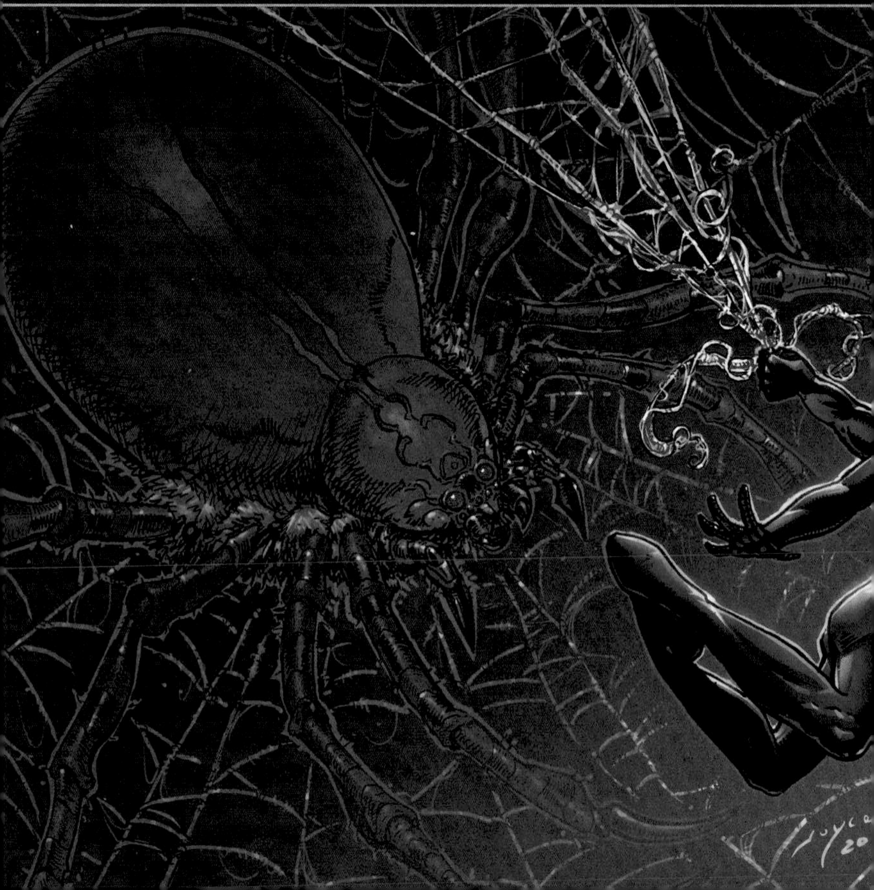

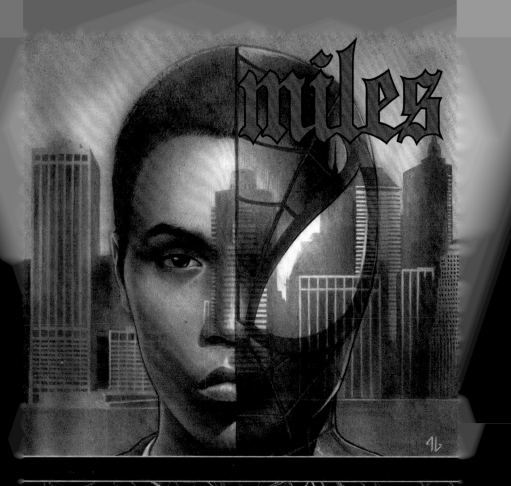

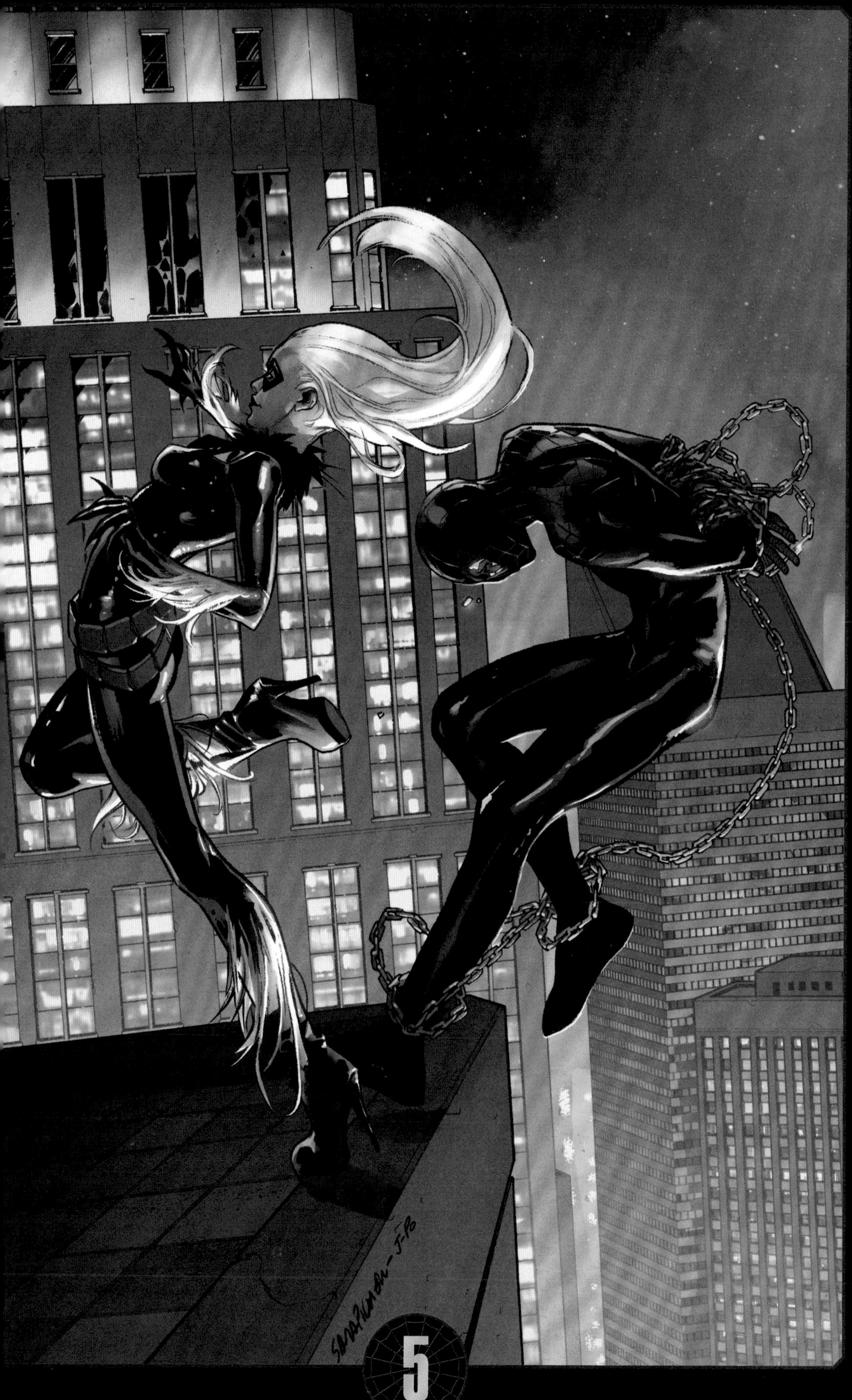

5

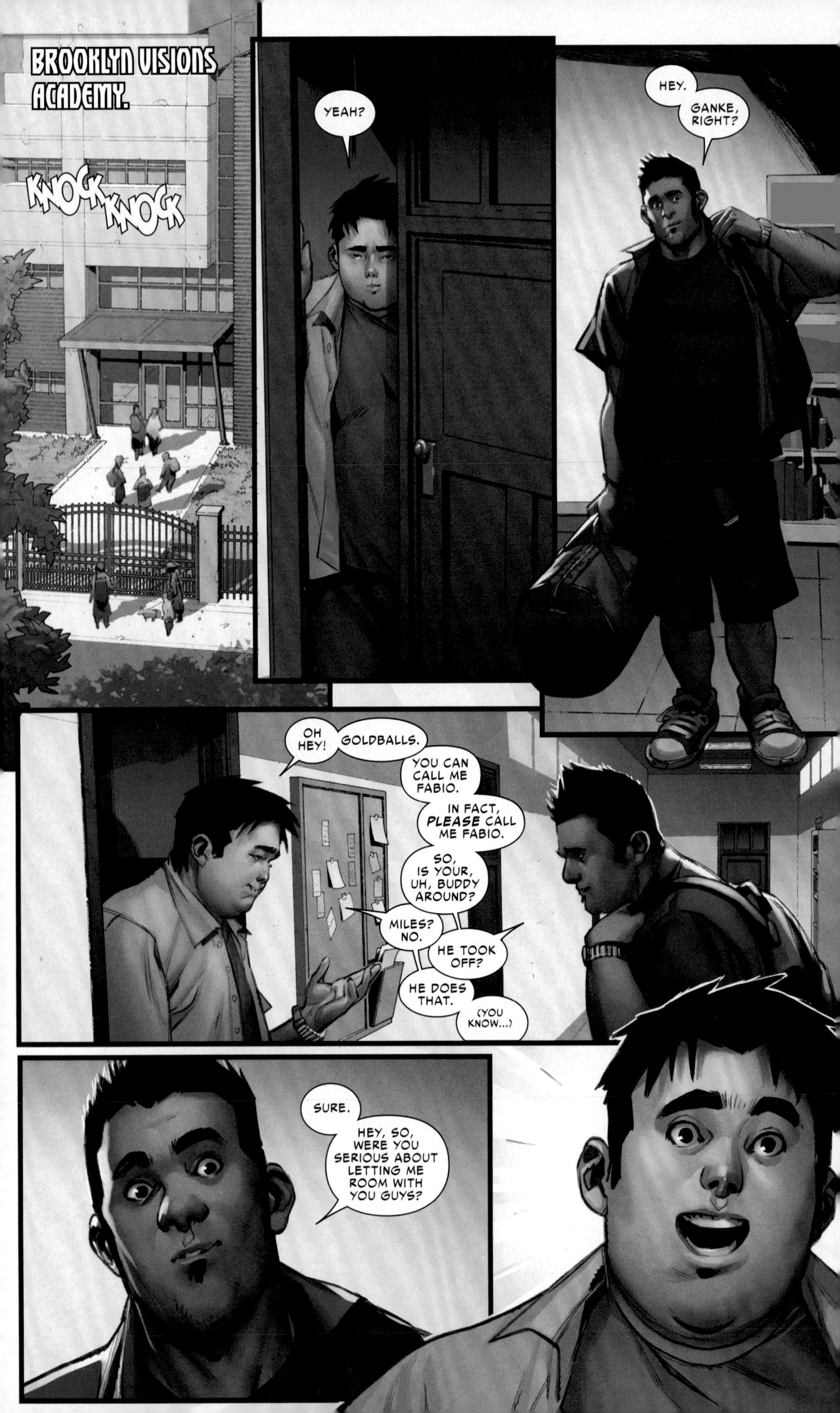
BROOKLYN VISIONS ACADEMY.
KNOCK KNOCK
YEAH?
HEY.
GANKE, RIGHT?
OH HEY!
GOLDBALLS.
YOU CAN CALL ME FABIO.
IN FACT, PLEASE CALL ME FABIO.
SO, IS YOUR, UH, BUDDY AROUND?
MILES? NO.
HE TOOK OFF?
HE DOES THAT.
(YOU KNOW...)
SURE.
HEY, SO, WERE YOU SERIOUS ABOUT LETTING ME ROOM WITH YOU GUYS?

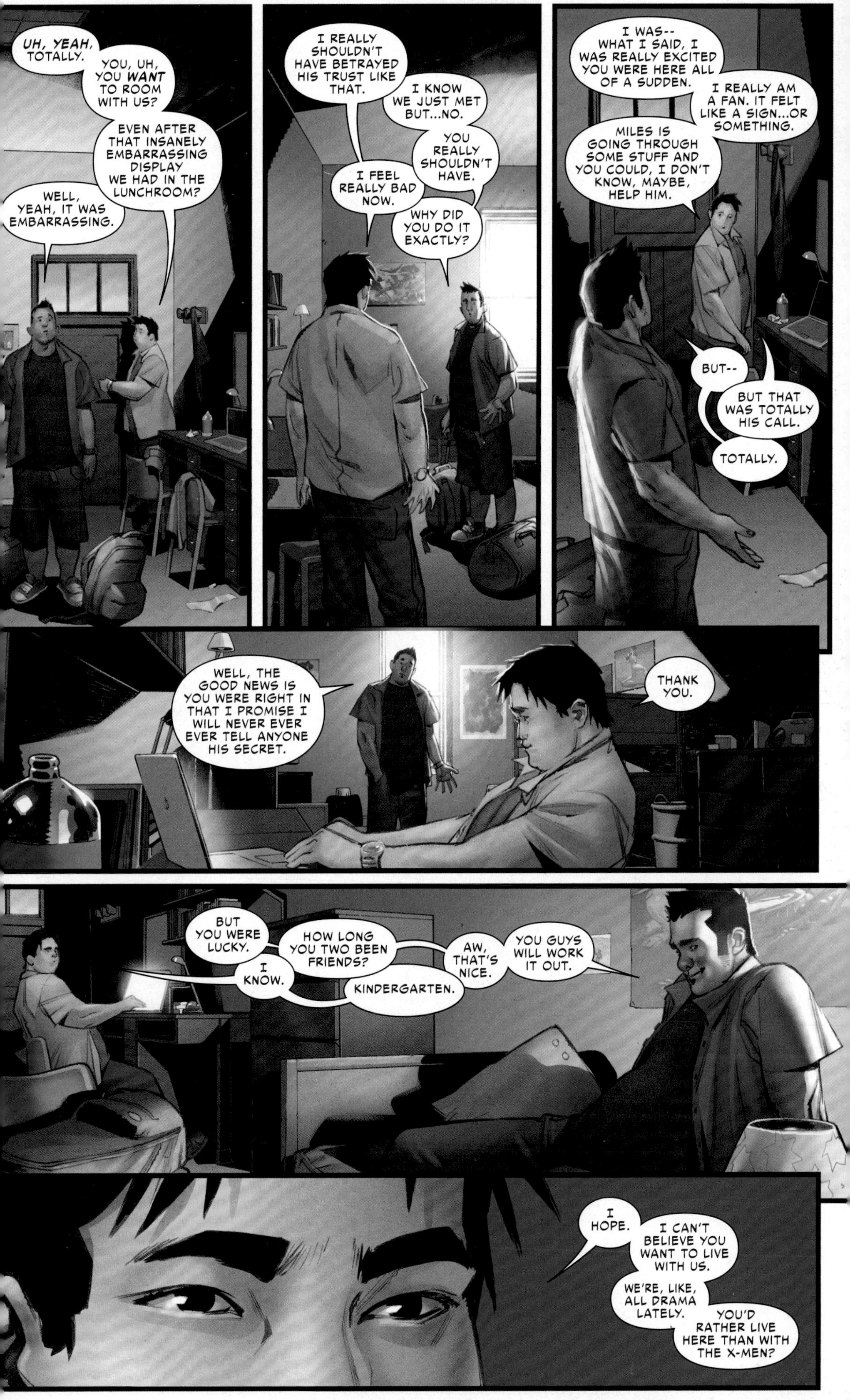
UH, YEAH, TOTALLY.
YOU, UH, YOU WANT TO ROOM WITH US?
EVEN AFTER THAT INSANELY EMBARRASSING DISPLAY WE HAD IN THE LUNCHROOM?
WELL, YEAH, IT WAS EMBARRASSING.
I REALLY SHOULDN'T HAVE BETRAYED HIS TRUST LIKE THAT.
I KNOW WE JUST MET BUT...NO.
YOU REALLY SHOULDN'T HAVE.
I FEEL REALLY BAD NOW.
WHY DID YOU DO IT EXACTLY?
I WAS-- WHAT I SAID, I WAS REALLY EXCITED YOU WERE HERE ALL OF A SUDDEN.
I REALLY AM A FAN. IT FELT LIKE A SIGN...OR SOMETHING.
MILES IS GOING THROUGH SOME STUFF AND YOU COULD, I DON'T KNOW, MAYBE, HELP HIM.
BUT--
BUT THAT WAS TOTALLY HIS CALL.
TOTALLY.
WELL, THE GOOD NEWS IS YOU WERE RIGHT IN THAT I PROMISE I WILL NEVER EVER EVER TELL ANYONE HIS SECRET.
THANK YOU.
BUT YOU WERE LUCKY.
I KNOW.
HOW LONG YOU TWO BEEN FRIENDS?
KINDERGARTEN.
AW, THAT'S NICE.
YOU GUYS WILL WORK IT OUT.
I HOPE.
I CAN'T BELIEVE YOU WANT TO LIVE WITH US.
WE'RE, LIKE, ALL DRAMA LATELY.
YOU'D RATHER LIVE HERE THAN WITH THE X-MEN?

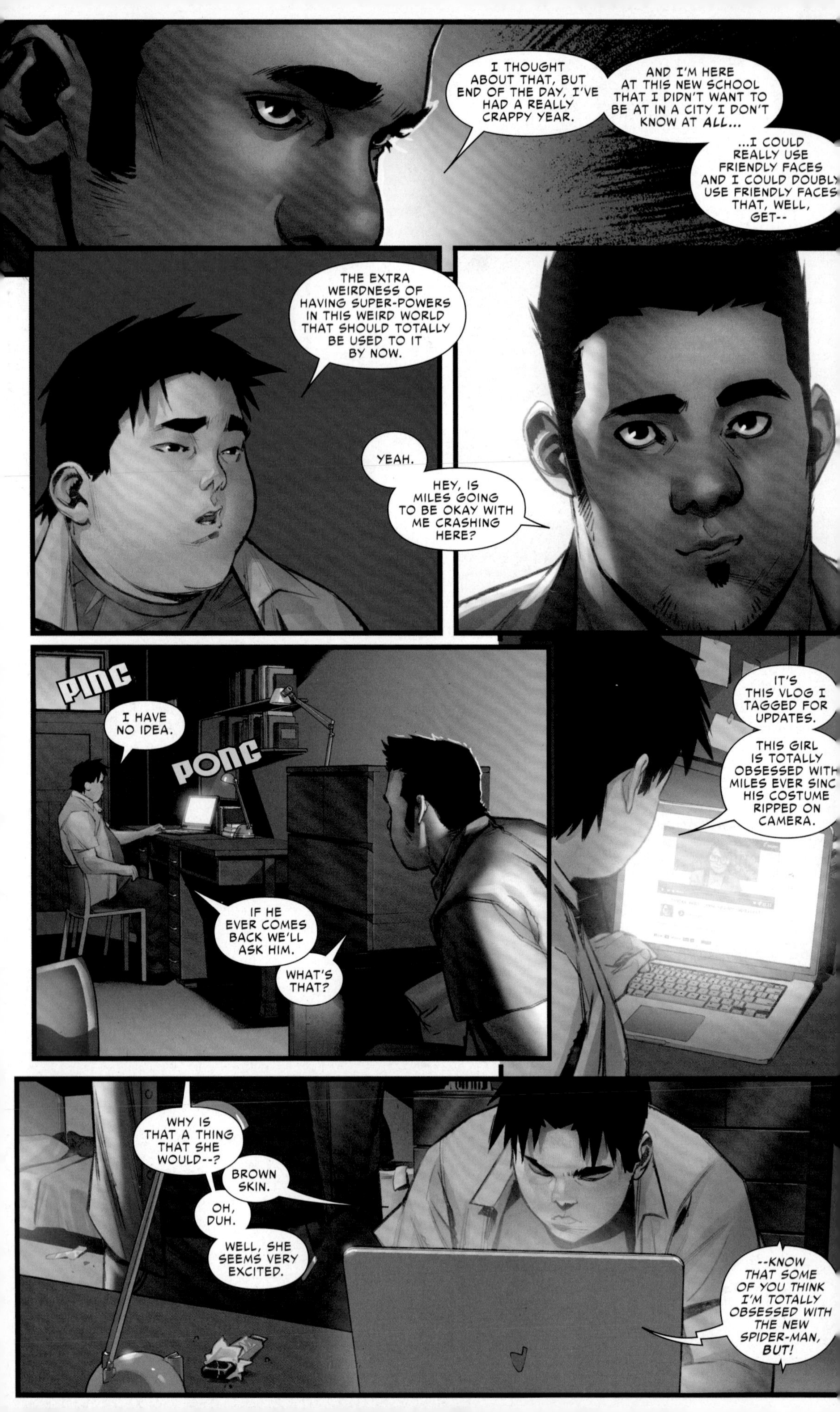
I THOUGHT ABOUT THAT, BUT END OF THE DAY, I'VE HAD A REALLY CRAPPY YEAR.
AND I'M HERE AT THIS NEW SCHOOL THAT I DIDN'T WANT TO BE AT IN A CITY I DON'T KNOW AT *ALL...*
...I COULD REALLY USE FRIENDLY FACES AND I COULD DOUBLY USE FRIENDLY FACES THAT, WELL, GET--
THE EXTRA WEIRDNESS OF HAVING SUPER-POWERS IN THIS WEIRD WORLD THAT SHOULD TOTALLY BE USED TO IT BY NOW.
YEAH.
HEY, IS MILES GOING TO BE OKAY WITH ME CRASHING HERE?
PING
I HAVE NO IDEA.
PONG
IF HE EVER COMES BACK WE'LL ASK HIM.
WHAT'S THAT?
IT'S THIS VLOG I TAGGED FOR UPDATES.
THIS GIRL IS TOTALLY OBSESSED WITH MILES EVER SINC HIS COSTUME RIPPED ON CAMERA.
WHY IS THAT A THING THAT SHE WOULD--?
BROWN SKIN.
OH, DUH.
WELL, SHE SEEMS VERY EXCITED.
--KNOW THAT SOME OF YOU THINK I'M TOTALLY OBSESSED WITH THE NEW SPIDER-MAN, BUT!

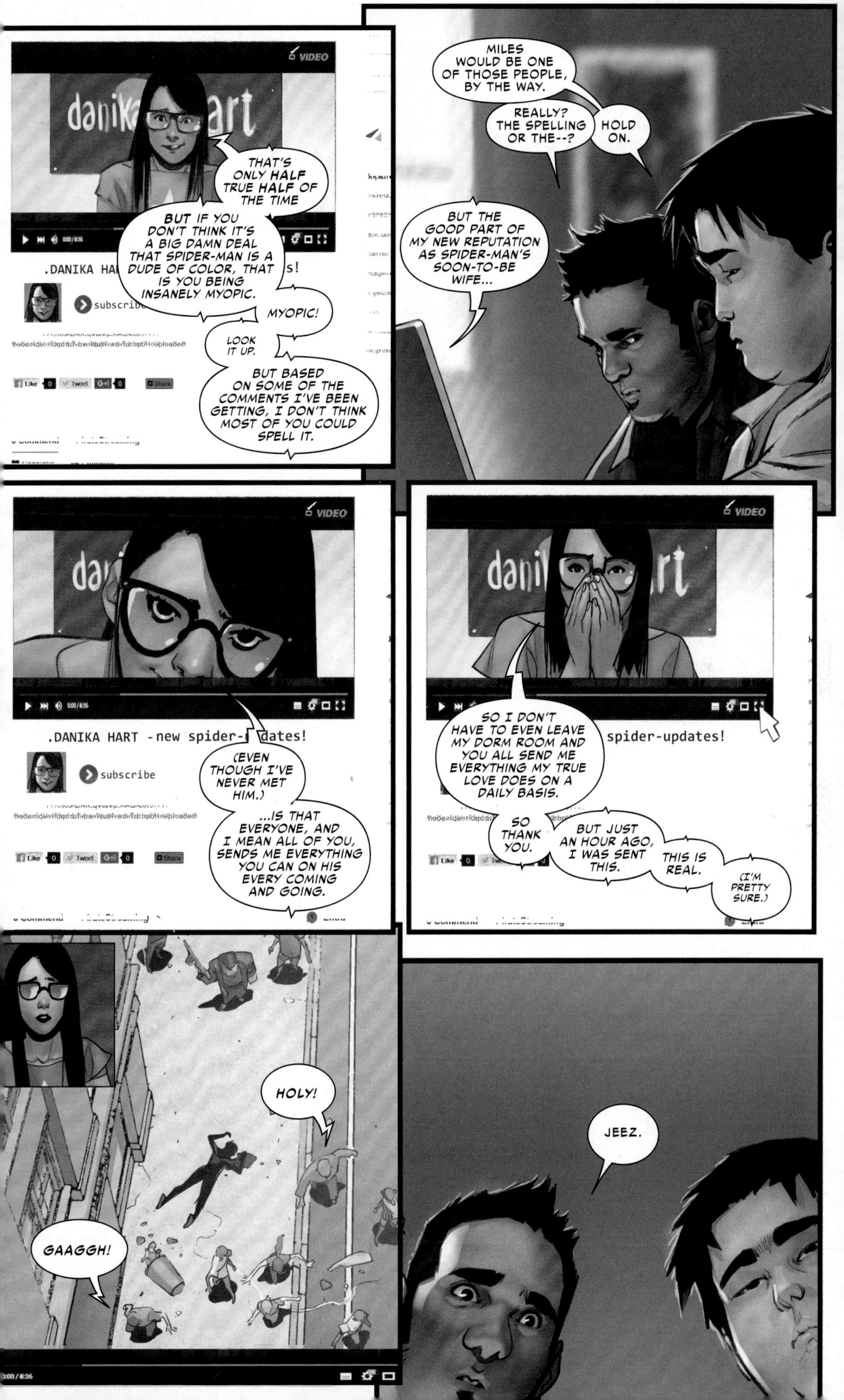
VIDEO
danika hart
THAT'S ONLY HALF TRUE HALF OF THE TIME
BUT IF YOU DON'T THINK IT'S A BIG DAMN DEAL THAT SPIDER-MAN IS A DUDE OF COLOR, THAT IS YOU BEING INSANELY MYOPIC.
MYOPIC!
LOOK IT UP.
BUT BASED ON SOME OF THE COMMENTS I'VE BEEN GETTING, I DON'T THINK MOST OF YOU COULD SPELL IT.
subscribe
MILES WOULD BE ONE OF THOSE PEOPLE, BY THE WAY.
REALLY? THE SPELLING OR THE--?
HOLD ON.
BUT THE GOOD PART OF MY NEW REPUTATION AS SPIDER-MAN'S SOON-TO-BE WIFE...
VIDEO
.DANIKA HART - new spider-updates!
subscribe
(EVEN THOUGH I'VE NEVER MET HIM.)
...IS THAT EVERYONE, AND I MEAN ALL OF YOU, SENDS ME EVERYTHING YOU CAN ON HIS EVERY COMING AND GOING.
VIDEO
spider-updates!
SO I DON'T HAVE TO EVEN LEAVE MY DORM ROOM AND YOU ALL SEND ME EVERYTHING MY TRUE LOVE DOES ON A DAILY BASIS.
SO THANK YOU.
BUT JUST AN HOUR AGO, I WAS SENT THIS.
THIS IS REAL.
(I'M PRETTY SURE.)
HOLY!
GAAGGH!
JEEZ.

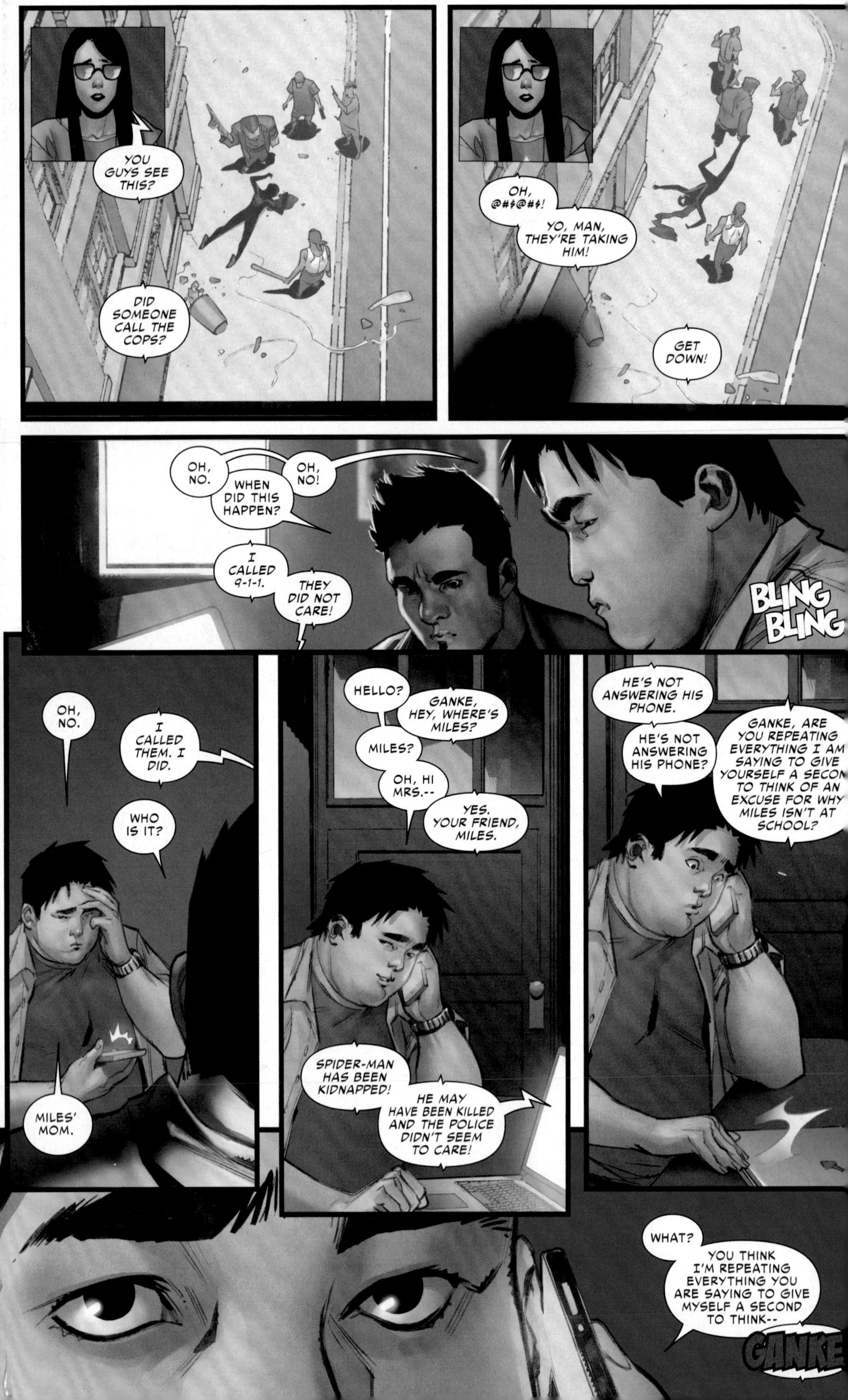
YOU GUYS SEE THIS?
DID SOMEONE CALL THE COPS?
OH, @#$@#$!
YO, MAN, THEY'RE TAKING HIM!
GET DOWN!
OH, NO.
OH, NO!
WHEN DID THIS HAPPEN?
I CALLED 9-1-1.
THEY DID NOT CARE!
BLING BLING
OH, NO.
I CALLED THEM. I DID.
WHO IS IT?
MILES' MOM.
HELLO?
GANKE, HEY, WHERE'S MILES?
MILES?
OH, HI MRS.--
YES. YOUR FRIEND, MILES.
SPIDER-MAN HAS BEEN KIDNAPPED!
HE MAY HAVE BEEN KILLED AND THE POLICE DIDN'T SEEM TO CARE!
HE'S NOT ANSWERING HIS PHONE.
HE'S NOT ANSWERING HIS PHONE?
GANKE, ARE YOU REPEATING EVERYTHING I AM SAYING TO GIVE YOURSELF A SECON TO THINK OF AN EXCUSE FOR WHY MILES ISN'T AT SCHOOL?
WHAT?
YOU THINK I'M REPEATING EVERYTHING YOU ARE SAYING TO GIVE MYSELF A SECOND TO THINK--
GANKE

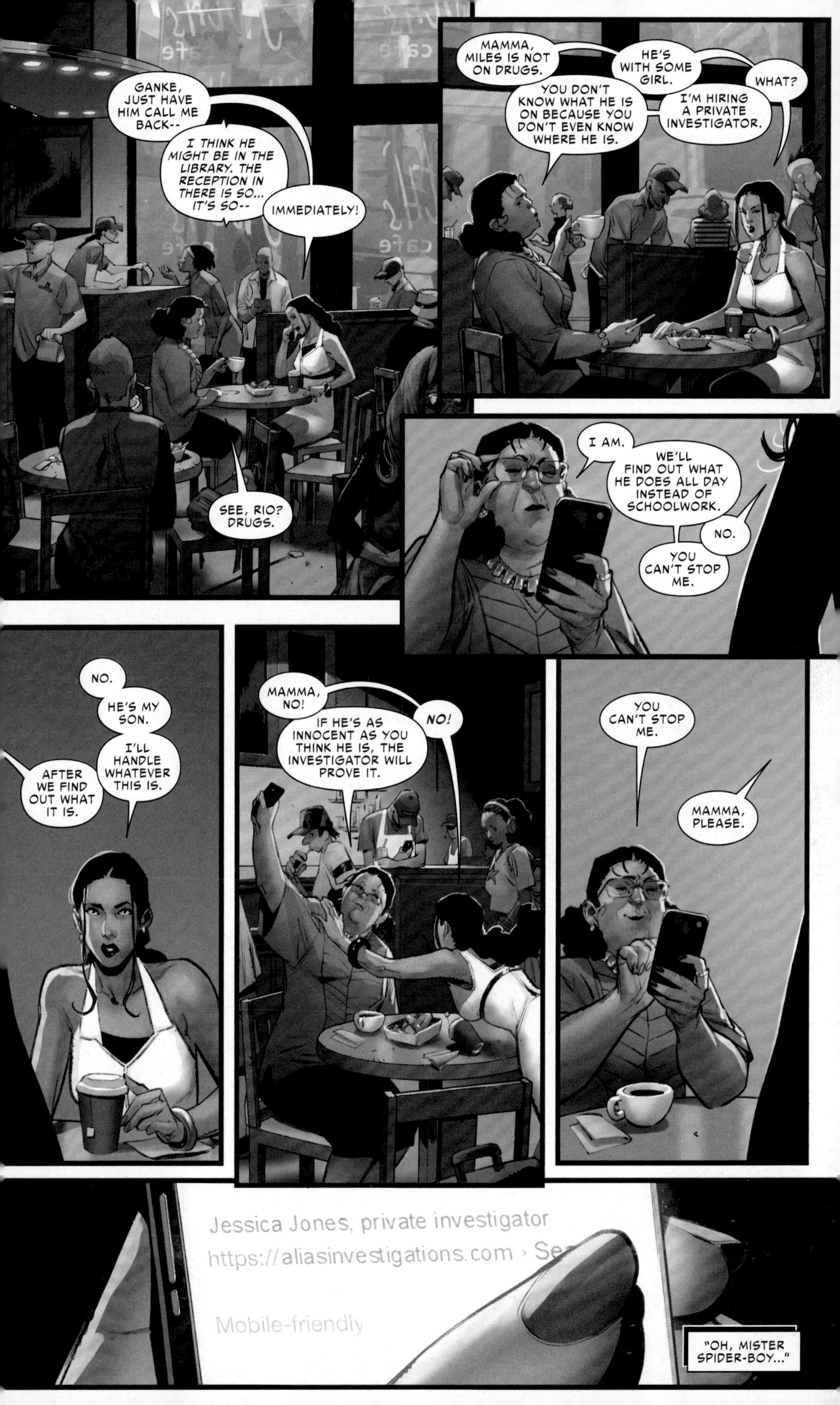
GANKE, JUST HAVE HIM CALL ME BACK--
I THINK HE MIGHT BE IN THE LIBRARY. THE RECEPTION IN THERE IS SO... IT'S SO--
IMMEDIATELY!
SEE, RIO? DRUGS.
MAMMA, MILES IS NOT ON DRUGS.
YOU DON'T KNOW WHAT HE IS ON BECAUSE YOU DON'T EVEN KNOW WHERE HE IS.
HE'S WITH SOME GIRL.
I'M HIRING A PRIVATE INVESTIGATOR.
WHAT?
I AM.
WE'LL FIND OUT WHAT HE DOES ALL DAY INSTEAD OF SCHOOLWORK.
NO.
YOU CAN'T STOP ME.
NO.
HE'S MY SON.
I'LL HANDLE WHATEVER THIS IS.
AFTER WE FIND OUT WHAT IT IS.
MAMMA, NO!
IF HE'S AS INNOCENT AS YOU THINK HE IS, THE INVESTIGATOR WILL PROVE IT.
NO!
YOU CAN'T STOP ME.
MAMMA, PLEASE.
Jessica Jones, private investigator
https://aliasinvestigations.com › Se
Mobile-friendly
"OH, MISTER SPIDER-BOY..."

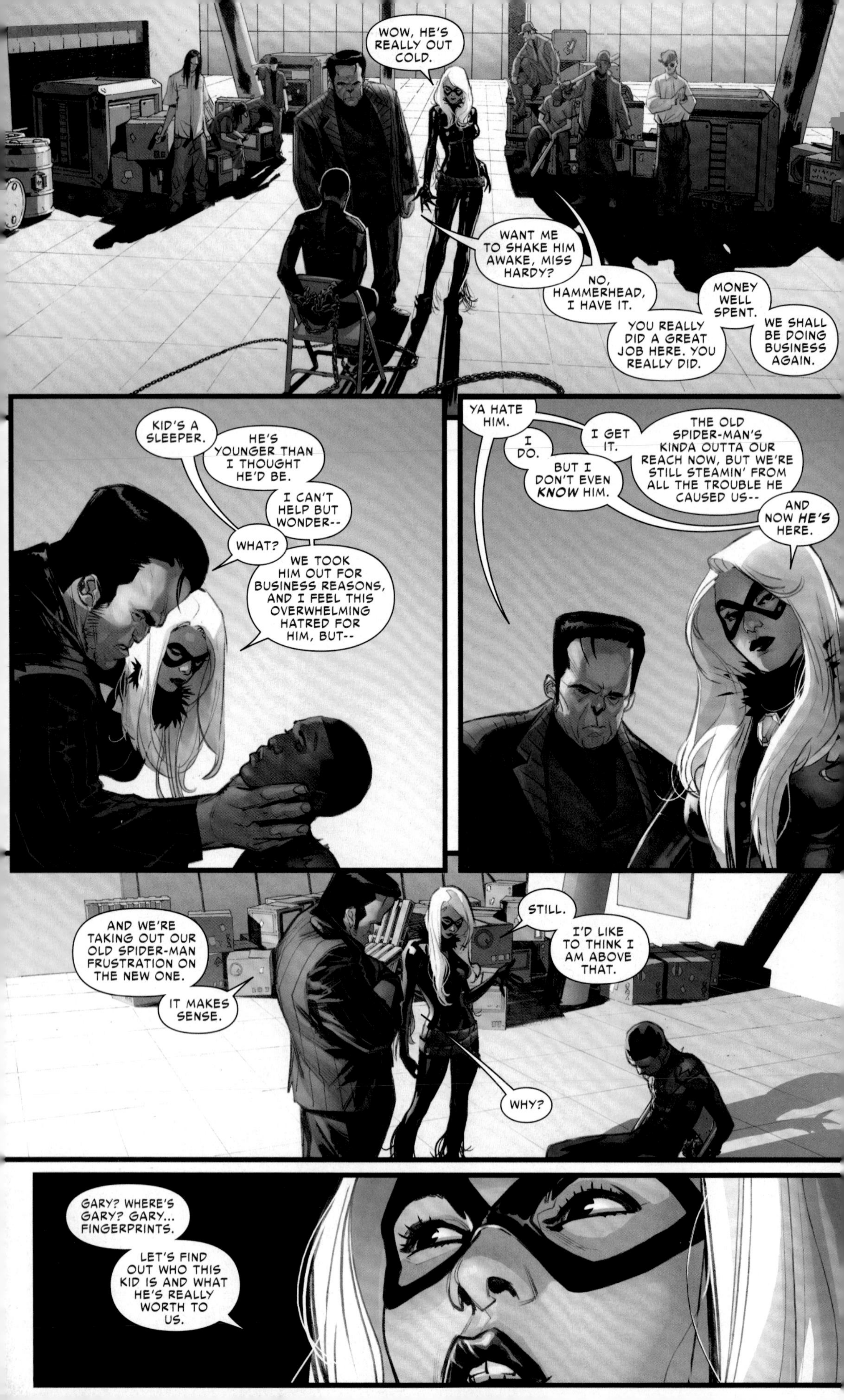
WOW, HE'S REALLY OUT COLD.
WANT ME TO SHAKE HIM AWAKE, MISS HARDY?
NO, HAMMERHEAD, I HAVE IT.
YOU REALLY DID A GREAT JOB HERE. YOU REALLY DID.
MONEY WELL SPENT.
WE SHALL BE DOING BUSINESS AGAIN.
KID'S A SLEEPER.
HE'S YOUNGER THAN I THOUGHT HE'D BE.
I CAN'T HELP BUT WONDER--
WHAT?
WE TOOK HIM OUT FOR BUSINESS REASONS, AND I FEEL THIS OVERWHELMING HATRED FOR HIM, BUT--
YA HATE HIM.
I DO.
I GET IT.
BUT I DON'T EVEN *KNOW* HIM.
THE OLD SPIDER-MAN'S KINDA OUTTA OUR REACH NOW, BUT WE'RE STILL STEAMIN' FROM ALL THE TROUBLE HE CAUSED US--
AND NOW *HE'S* HERE.
AND WE'RE TAKING OUT OUR OLD SPIDER-MAN FRUSTRATION ON THE NEW ONE.
IT MAKES SENSE.
STILL.
I'D LIKE TO THINK I AM ABOVE THAT.
WHY?
GARY? WHERE'S GARY? GARY... FINGERPRINTS.
LET'S FIND OUT WHO THIS KID IS AND WHAT HE'S REALLY WORTH TO US.

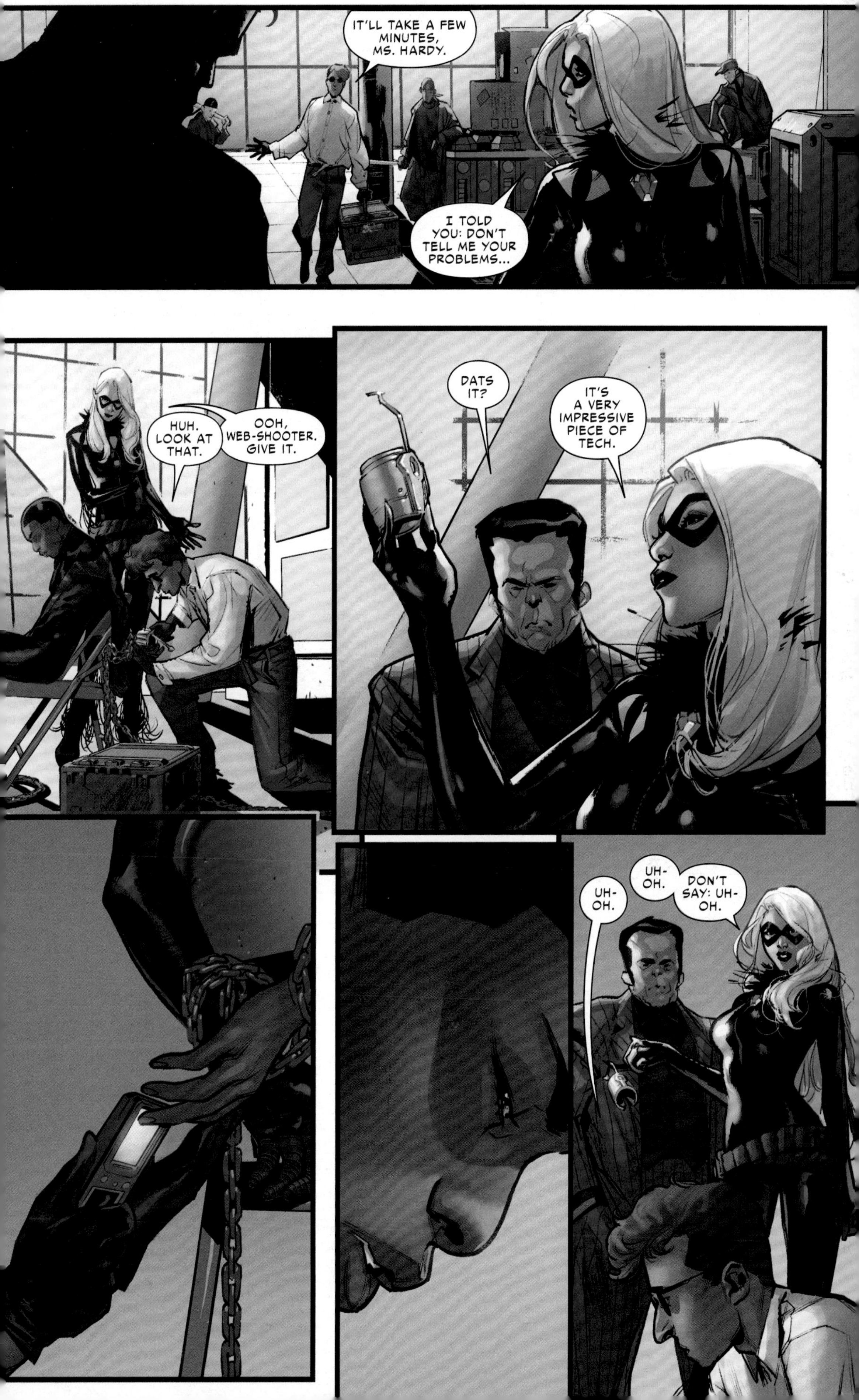
IT'LL TAKE A FEW MINUTES, MS. HARDY.
I TOLD YOU: DON'T TELL ME YOUR PROBLEMS...
HUH. LOOK AT THAT.
OOH, WEB-SHOOTER. GIVE IT.
DATS IT?
IT'S A VERY IMPRESSIVE PIECE OF TECH.
UH-OH.
UH-OH.
DON'T SAY: UH-OH.

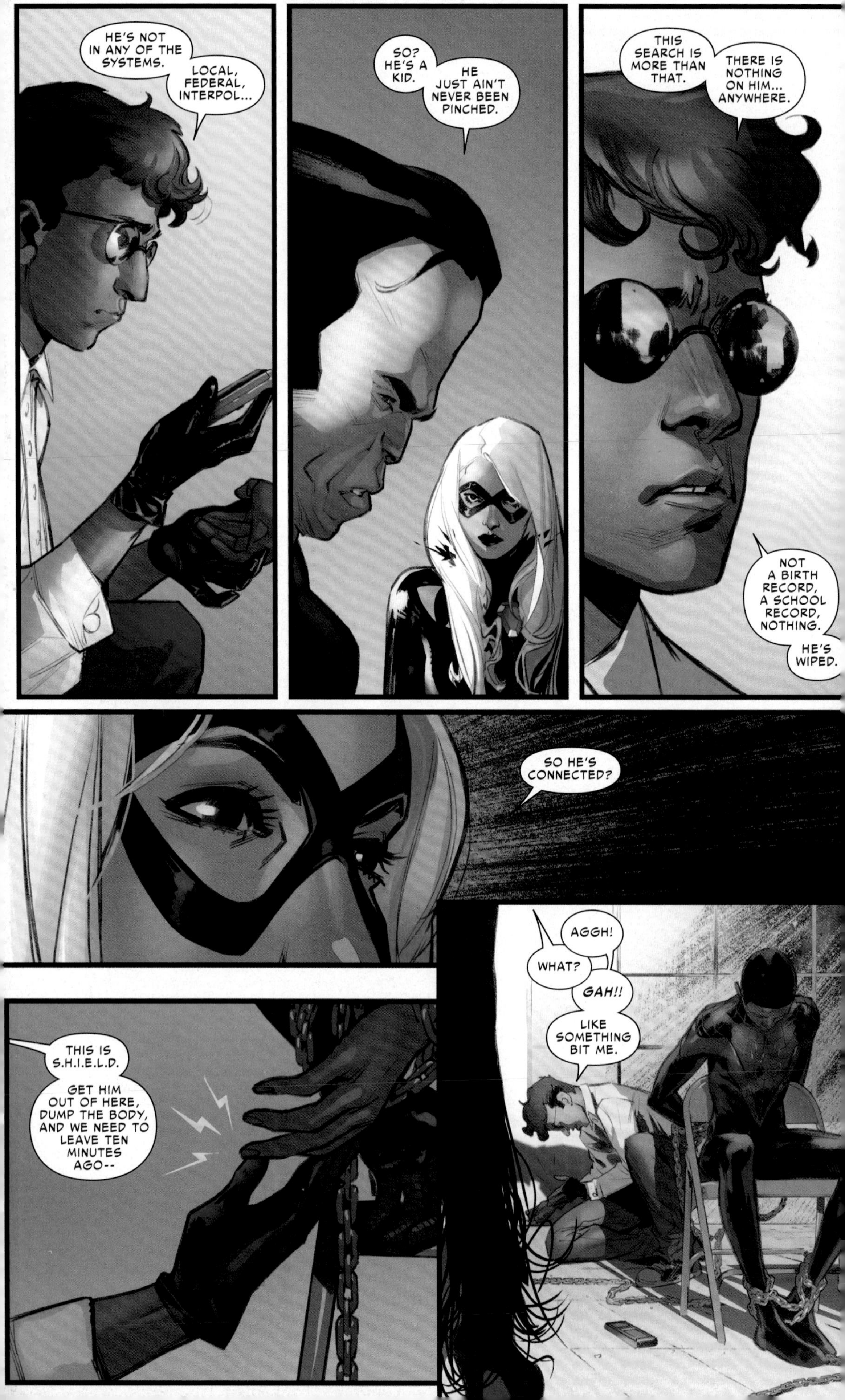

HE'S NOT IN ANY OF THE SYSTEMS.
LOCAL, FEDERAL, INTERPOL...
SO? HE'S A KID.
HE JUST AIN'T NEVER BEEN PINCHED.
THIS SEARCH IS MORE THAN THAT.
THERE IS NOTHING ON HIM... ANYWHERE.
NOT A BIRTH RECORD, A SCHOOL RECORD, NOTHING.
HE'S WIPED.
SO HE'S CONNECTED?
THIS IS S.H.I.E.L.D.
GET HIM OUT OF HERE, DUMP THE BODY, AND WE NEED TO LEAVE TEN MINUTES AGO--
AGGH!
WHAT?
GAH!!
LIKE SOMETHING BIT ME.

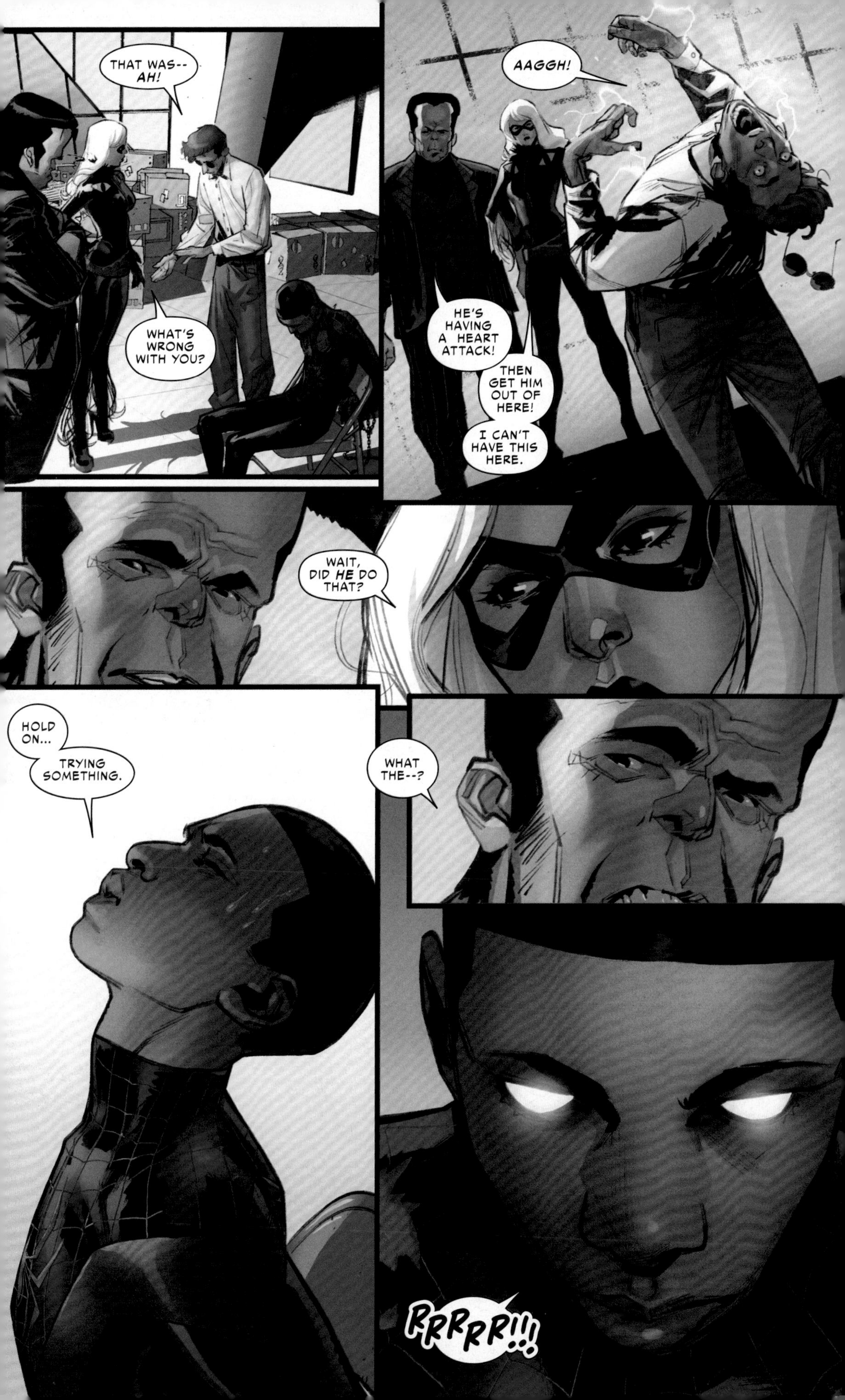
THAT WAS-- AH!
WHAT'S WRONG WITH YOU?
AAGGH!
HE'S HAVING A HEART ATTACK!
THEN GET HIM OUT OF HERE!
I CAN'T HAVE THIS HERE.
WAIT, DID HE DO THAT?
HOLD ON...
TRYING SOMETHING.
WHAT THE--?
RRRRR!!!

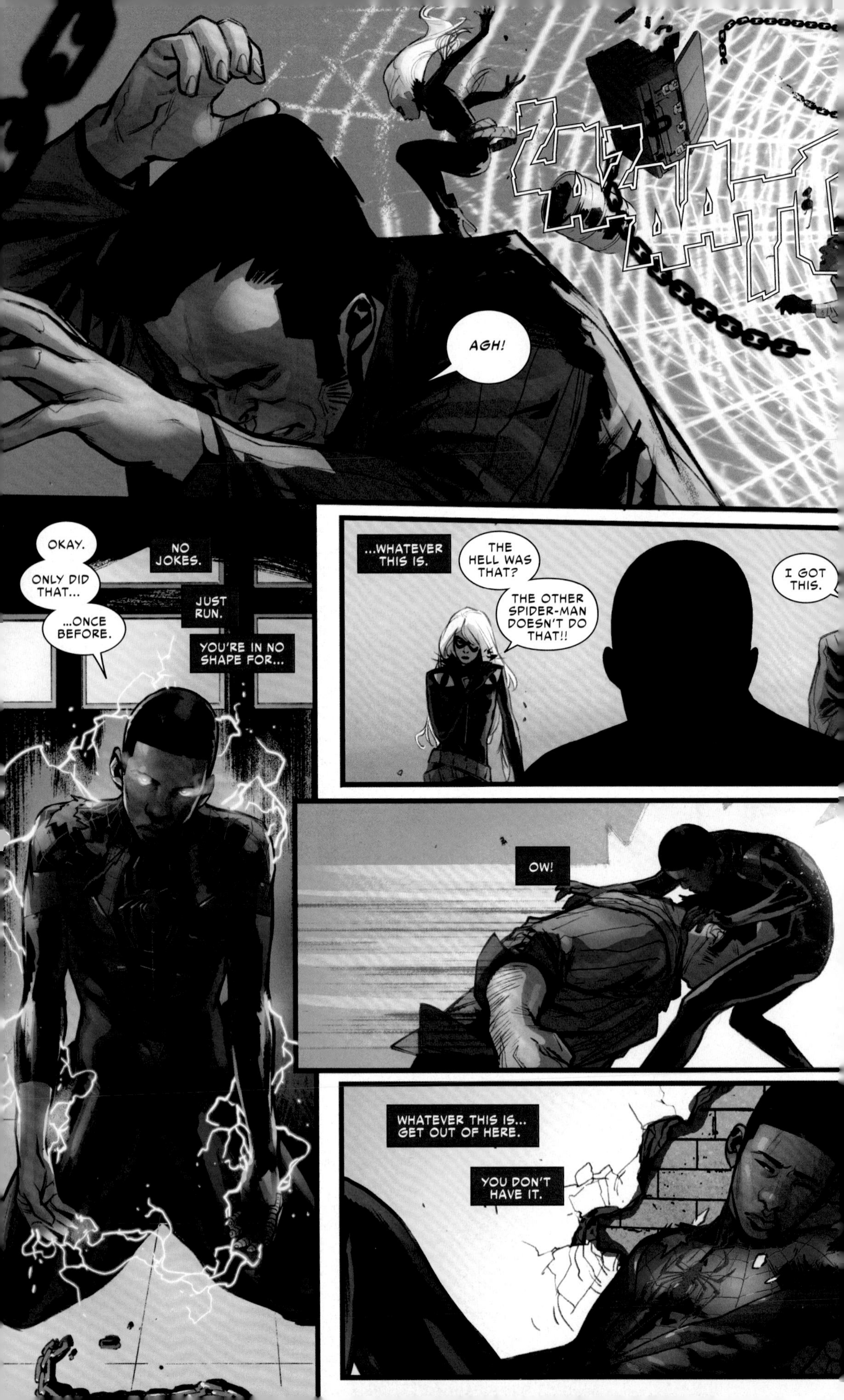
AGH!
OKAY.
ONLY DID THAT...
...ONCE BEFORE.
NO JOKES.
JUST RUN.
YOU'RE IN NO SHAPE FOR...
...WHATEVER THIS IS.
THE HELL WAS THAT?
THE OTHER SPIDER-MAN DOESN'T DO THAT!!
I GOT THIS.
OW!
WHATEVER THIS IS... GET OUT OF HERE.
YOU DON'T HAVE IT.

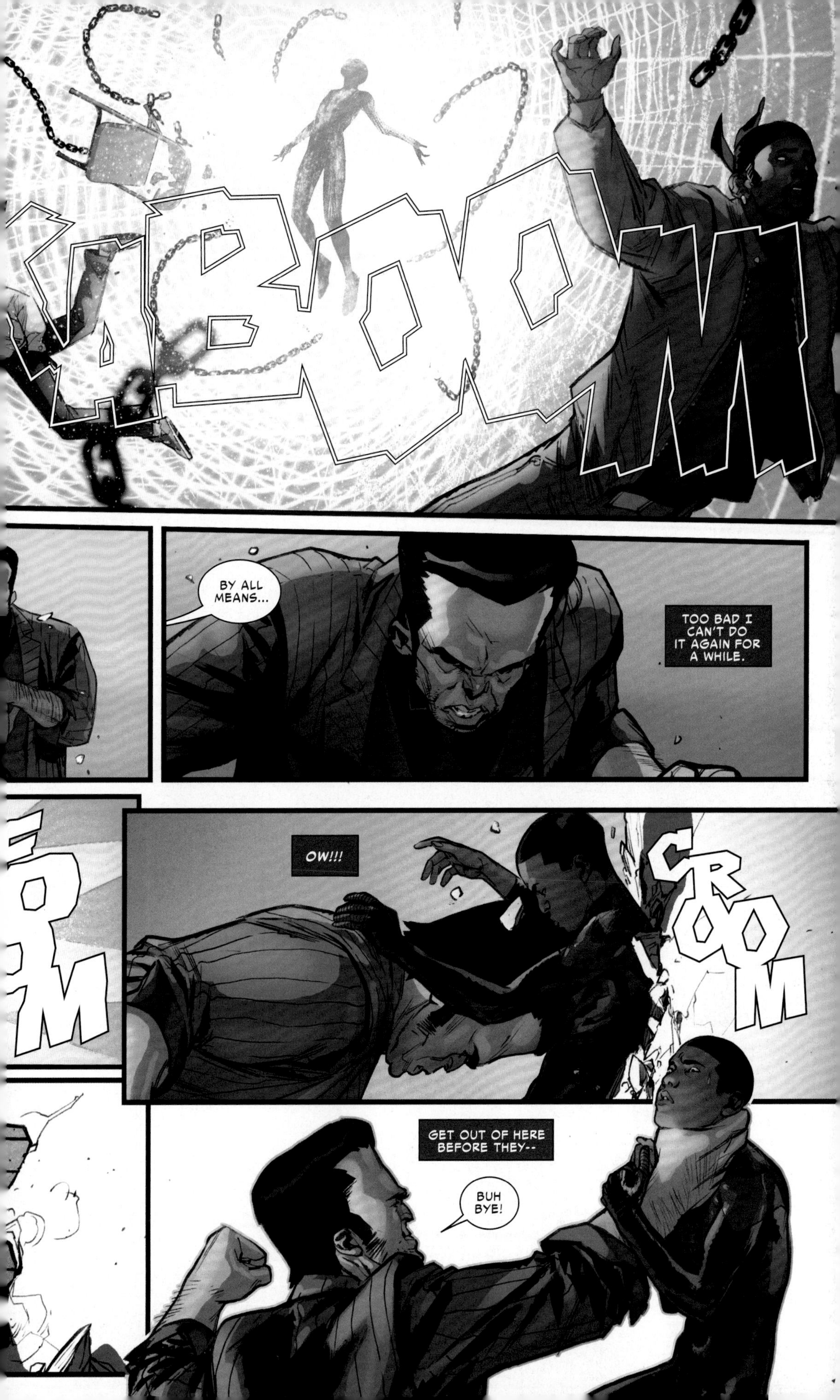

KABOOM
BY ALL MEANS...
TOO BAD I CAN'T DO IT AGAIN FOR A WHILE.
OW!!!
CROOM
GET OUT OF HERE BEFORE THEY--
BUH BYE!

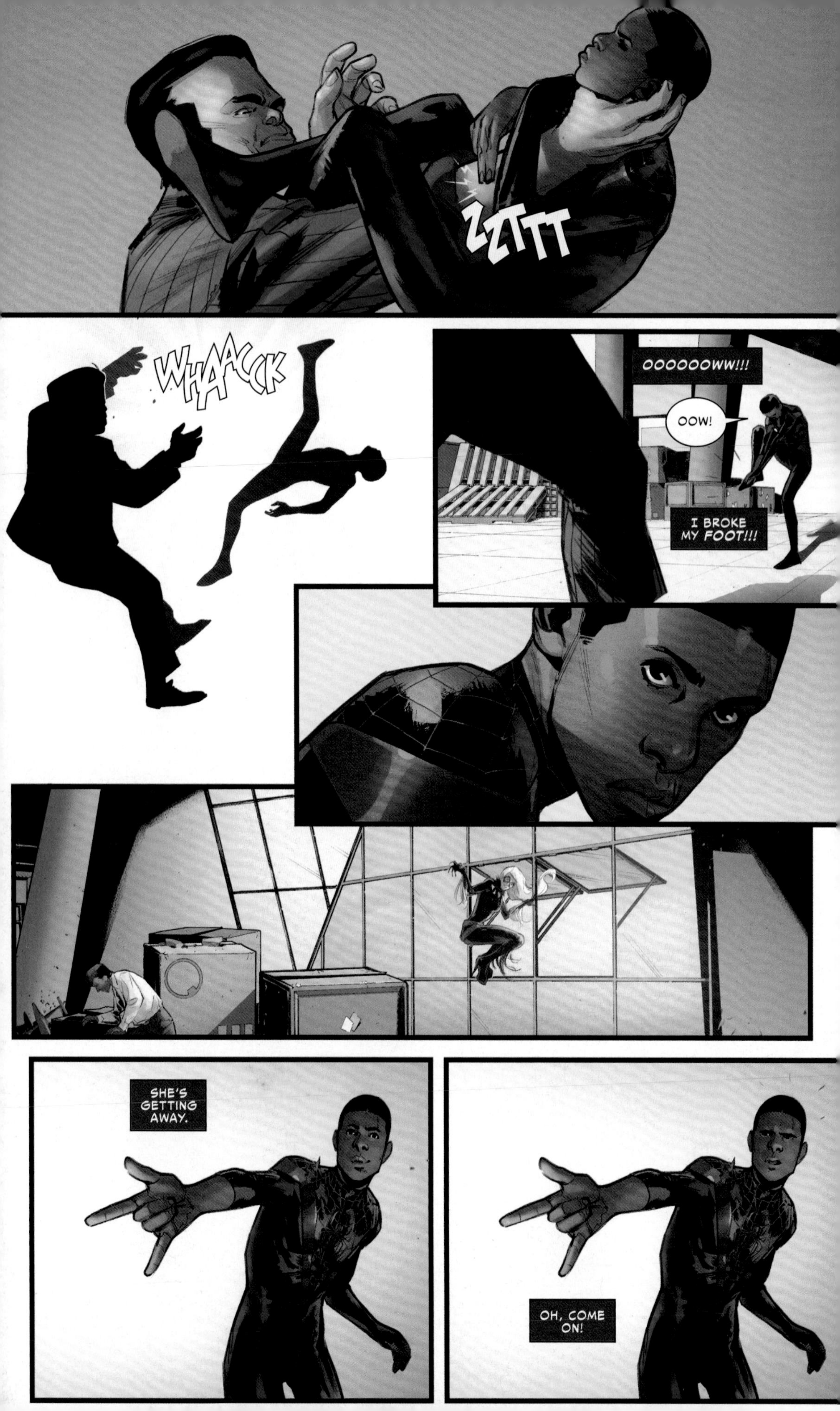
ZZTTT
WHAACCK
OOOOOOWW!!!
OOW!
I BROKE MY FOOT!!!
SHE'S GETTING AWAY.
OH, COME ON!

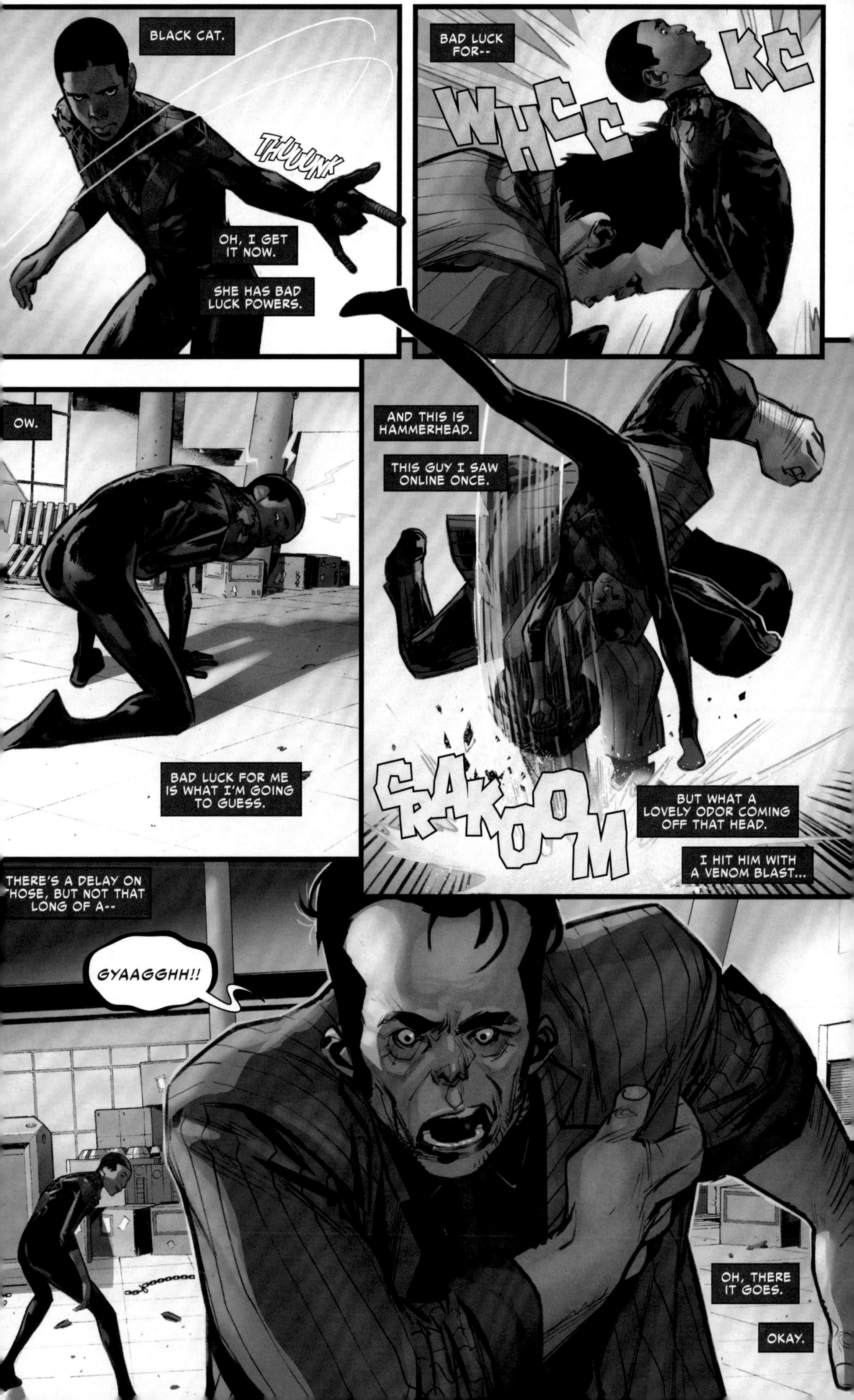
BLACK CAT.
THUUUNK
OH, I GET IT NOW.
SHE HAS BAD LUCK POWERS.
BAD LUCK FOR--
WHCCKC
OW.
BAD LUCK FOR ME IS WHAT I'M GOING TO GUESS.
AND THIS IS HAMMERHEAD.
THIS GUY I SAW ONLINE ONCE.
CRAKOOOM
BUT WHAT A LOVELY ODOR COMING OFF THAT HEAD.
I HIT HIM WITH A VENOM BLAST...
THERE'S A DELAY ON THOSE, BUT NOT THAT LONG OF A--
GYAAGGHH!!
OH, THERE IT GOES.
OKAY.

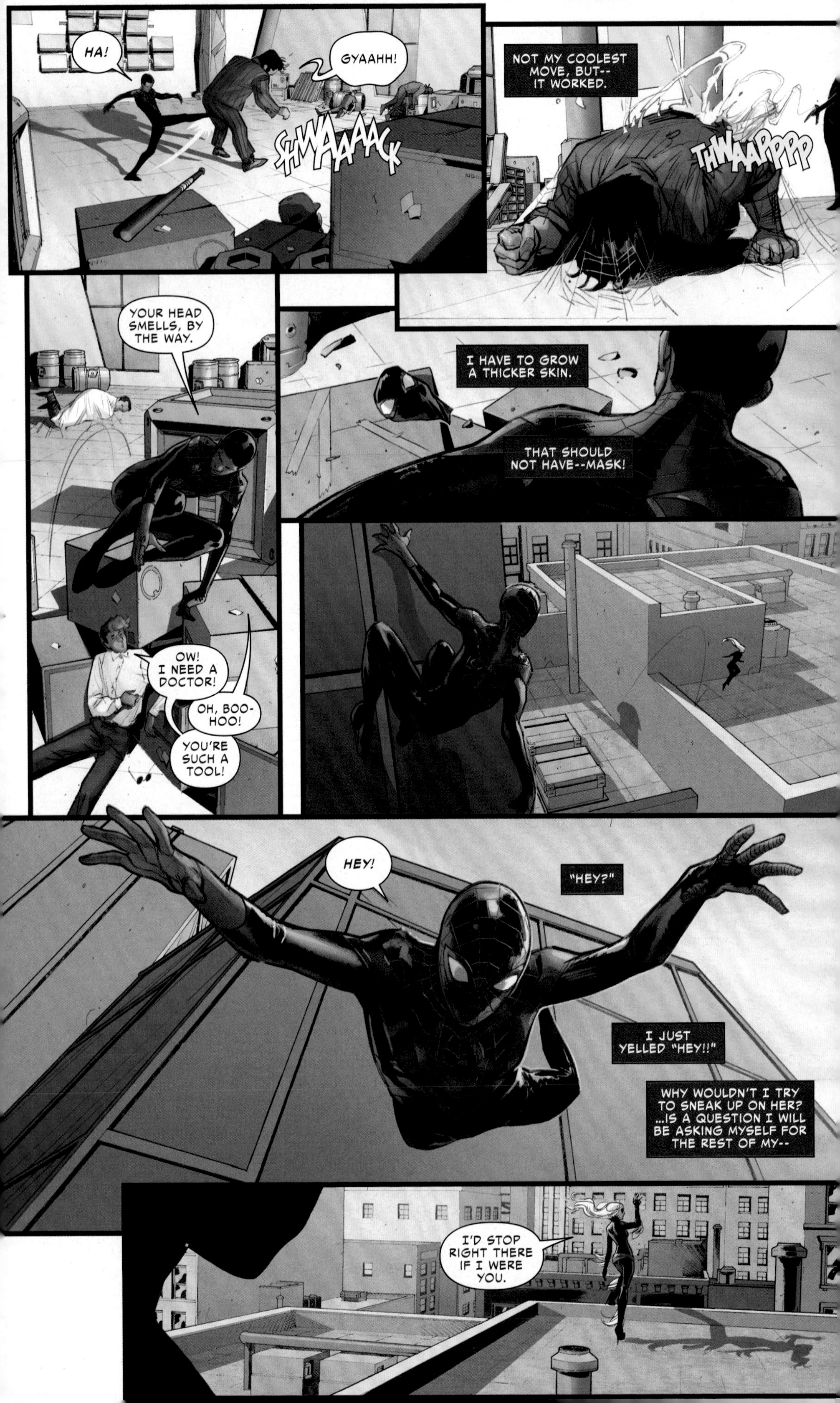
HA!
GYAAHH!
SHWAAAACK
NOT MY COOLEST MOVE, BUT-- IT WORKED.
THWAAPPPP
YOUR HEAD SMELLS, BY THE WAY.
OW! I NEED A DOCTOR!
OH, BOO-HOO!
YOU'RE SUCH A TOOL!
I HAVE TO GROW A THICKER SKIN.
THAT SHOULD NOT HAVE--MASK!
HEY!
"HEY?"
I JUST YELLED "HEY!!"
WHY WOULDN'T I TRY TO SNEAK UP ON HER? ...IS A QUESTION I WILL BE ASKING MYSELF FOR THE REST OF MY--
I'D STOP RIGHT THERE IF I WERE YOU.

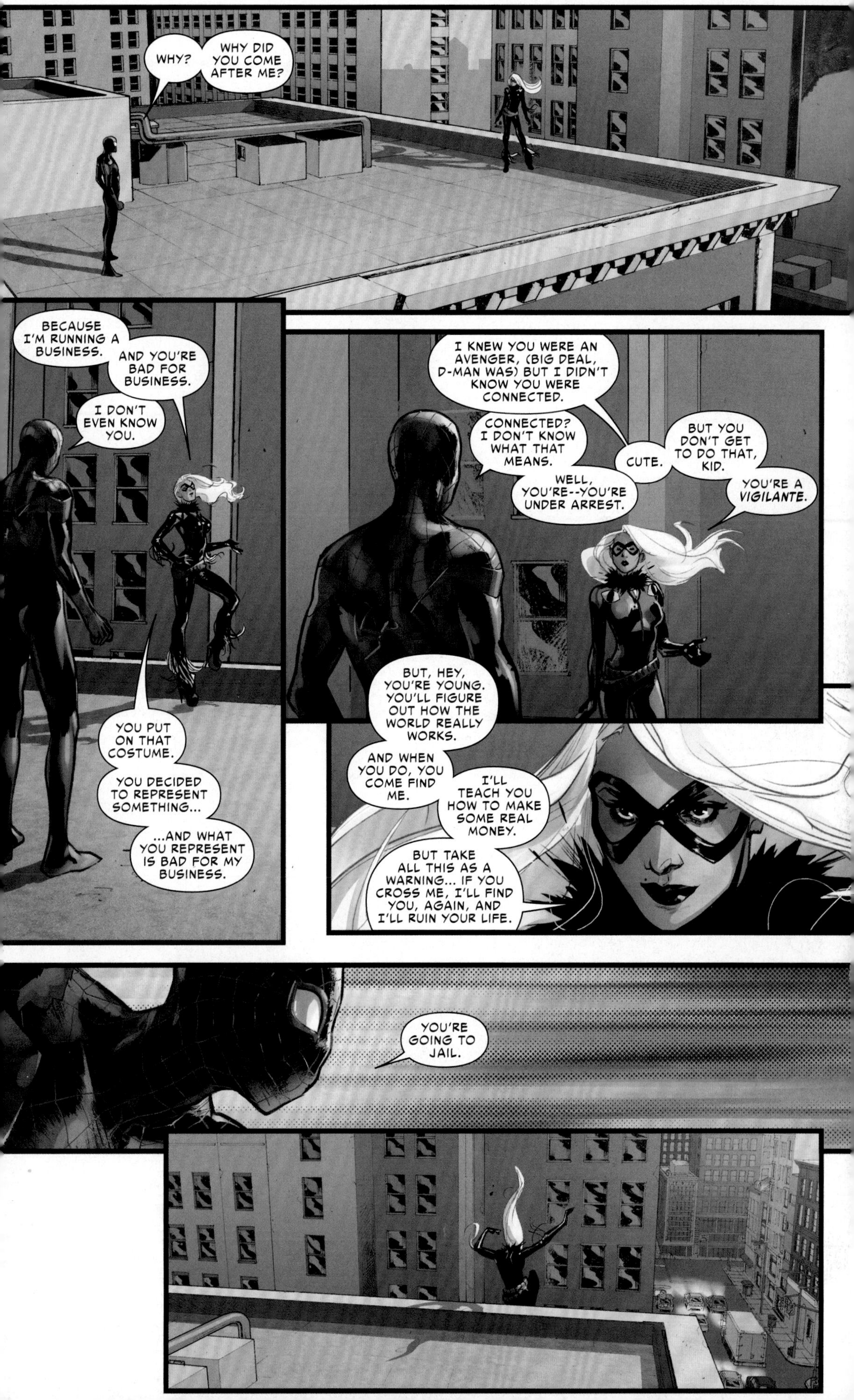

WHY?
WHY DID YOU COME AFTER ME?
BECAUSE I'M RUNNING A BUSINESS.
AND YOU'RE BAD FOR BUSINESS.
I DON'T EVEN KNOW YOU.
YOU PUT ON THAT COSTUME.
YOU DECIDED TO REPRESENT SOMETHING...
...AND WHAT YOU REPRESENT IS BAD FOR MY BUSINESS.
I KNEW YOU WERE AN AVENGER, (BIG DEAL, D-MAN WAS) BUT I DIDN'T KNOW YOU WERE CONNECTED.
CONNECTED? I DON'T KNOW WHAT THAT MEANS.
WELL, YOU'RE--YOU'RE UNDER ARREST.
CUTE.
BUT YOU DON'T GET TO DO THAT, KID.
YOU'RE A *VIGILANTE.*
BUT, HEY, YOU'RE YOUNG. YOU'LL FIGURE OUT HOW THE WORLD REALLY WORKS.
AND WHEN YOU DO, YOU COME FIND ME.
I'LL TEACH YOU HOW TO MAKE SOME REAL MONEY.
BUT TAKE ALL THIS AS A WARNING... IF YOU CROSS ME, I'LL FIND YOU, AGAIN, AND I'LL RUIN YOUR LIFE.
YOU'RE GOING TO JAIL.

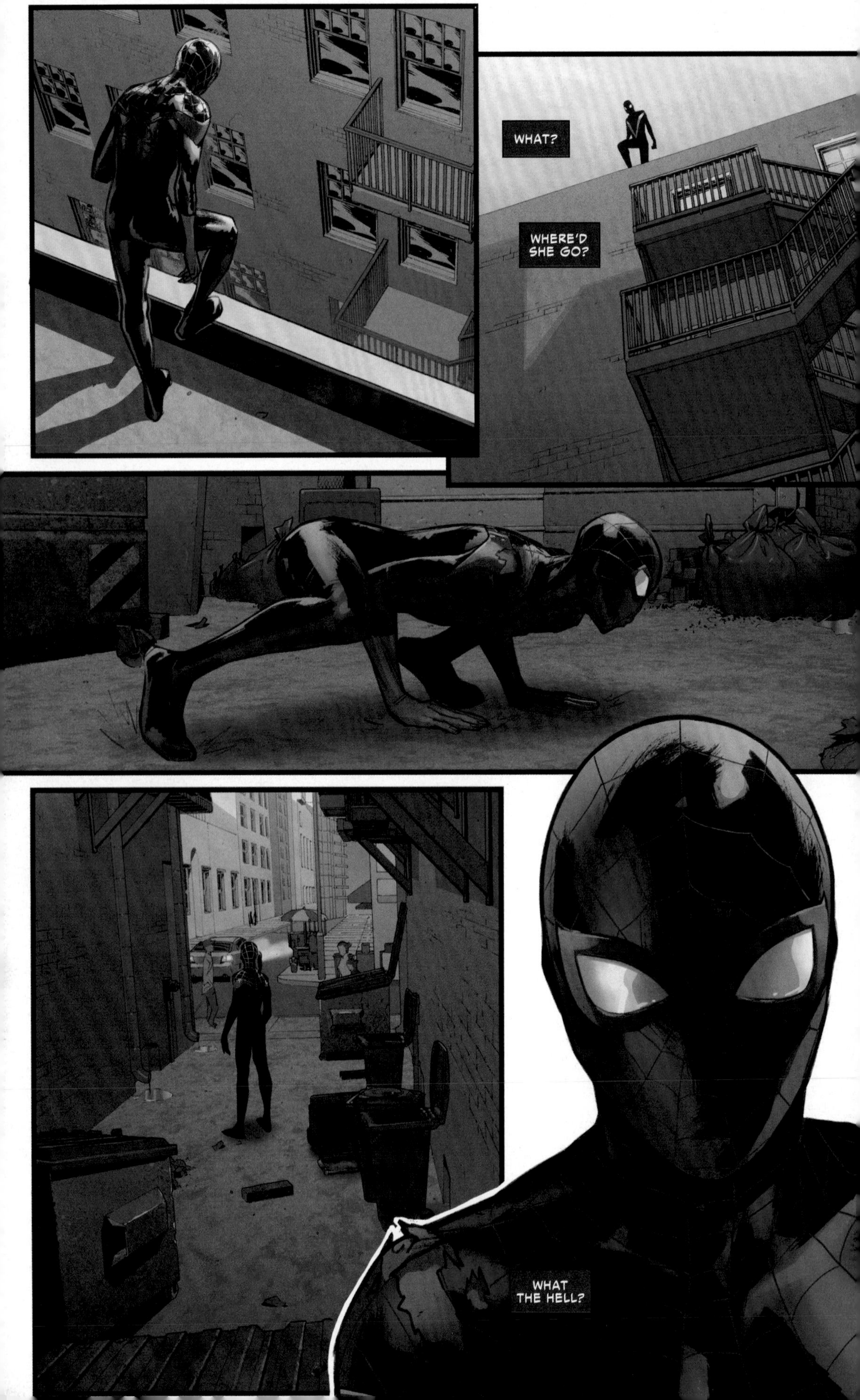
WHAT?
WHERE'D SHE GO?
WHAT THE HELL?

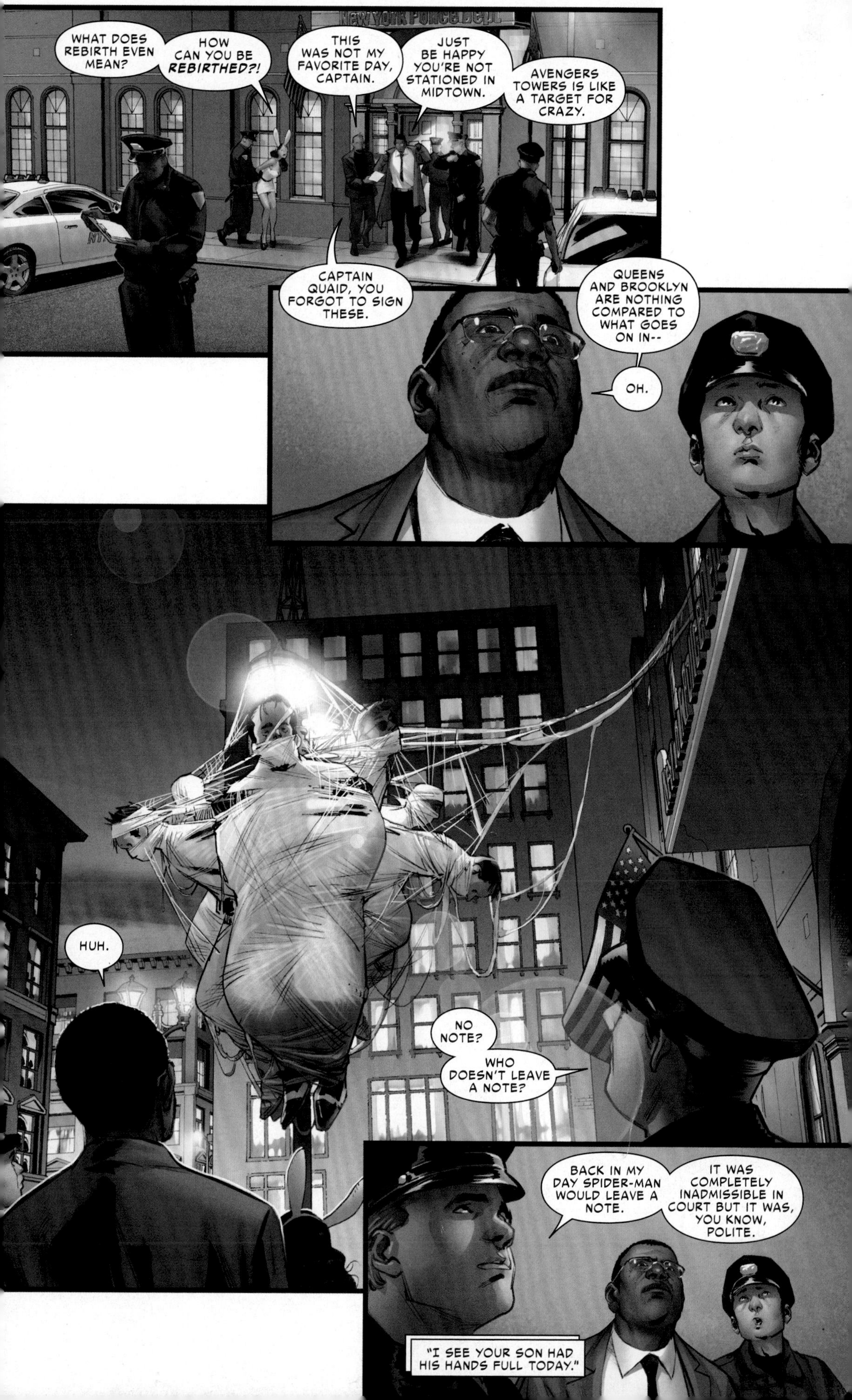

WHAT DOES REBIRTH EVEN MEAN?
HOW CAN YOU BE REBIRTHED?!
THIS WAS NOT MY FAVORITE DAY, CAPTAIN.
JUST BE HAPPY YOU'RE NOT STATIONED IN MIDTOWN.
AVENGERS TOWERS IS LIKE A TARGET FOR CRAZY.
CAPTAIN QUAID, YOU FORGOT TO SIGN THESE.
QUEENS AND BROOKLYN ARE NOTHING COMPARED TO WHAT GOES ON IN--
OH.
HUH.
NO NOTE?
WHO DOESN'T LEAVE A NOTE?
BACK IN MY DAY SPIDER-MAN WOULD LEAVE A NOTE.
IT WAS COMPLETELY INADMISSIBLE IN COURT BUT IT WAS, YOU KNOW, POLITE.
"I SEE YOUR SON HAD HIS HANDS FULL TODAY."

YOU WOULD KNOW BETTER THAN ME.

I THOUGHT YOU AND YOUR SON WERE CLOSE.

I THOUGHT HE CONFIDED IN YOU.

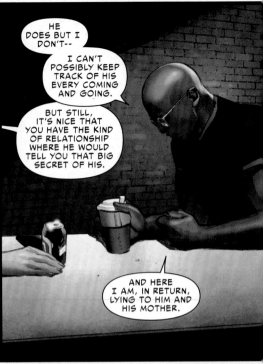

HE DOES BUT I DON'T--

I CAN'T POSSIBLY KEEP TRACK OF HIS EVERY COMING AND GOING.

BUT STILL, IT'S NICE THAT YOU HAVE THE KIND OF RELATIONSHIP WHERE HE WOULD TELL YOU THAT BIG SECRET OF HIS.

AND HERE I AM, IN RETURN, LYING TO HIM AND HIS MOTHER.

BUT YOU KNOW THAT'S THE DEAL.

IT'S THE SAME FOR ALL OF US.

IF YOU TELL THEM, YOU PUT THEM IN DANGER. YOU COMPROMISE YOUR SITUATION.

I KNOW.

HE'S A GOOD KID, JEFFERSON.

THE AVENGERS SPEAK SO HIGHLY OF HIM.

SO WE HAVE A DEAL, MISS HILL?

YES.

WE WILL DO WHAT WE CAN TO PROTECT HIM. I ALREADY STARTED THE BALL ROLLING, AGENT.

"AGENT."

WELCOME BACK TO S.H.I.E.L.D.

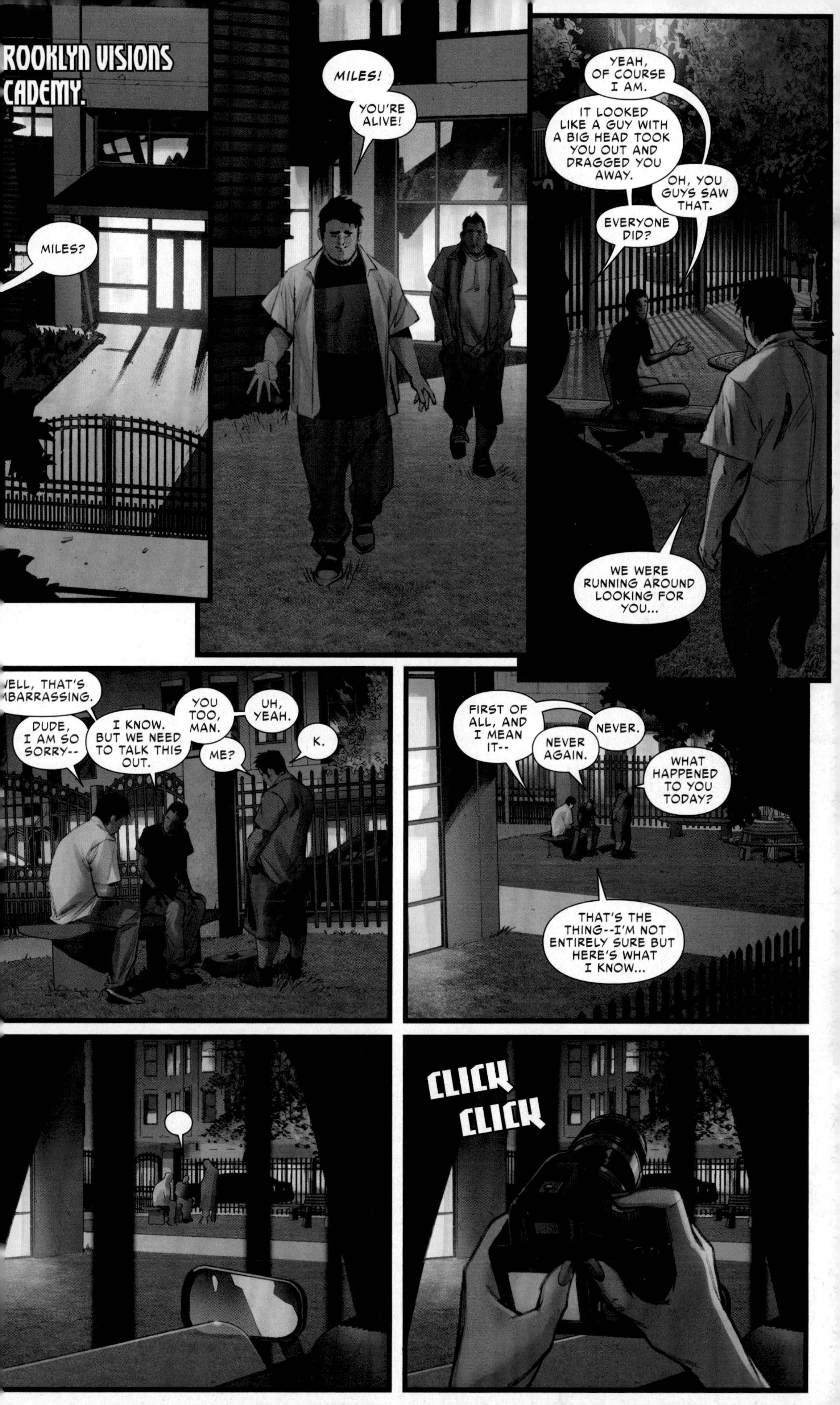
ROOKLYN VISIONS CADEMY.
MILES?
MILES!
YOU'RE ALIVE!
YEAH, OF COURSE I AM.
IT LOOKED LIKE A GUY WITH A BIG HEAD TOOK YOU OUT AND DRAGGED YOU AWAY.
OH, YOU GUYS SAW THAT.
EVERYONE DID?
WE WERE RUNNING AROUND LOOKING FOR YOU...
WELL, THAT'S MBARRASSING.
DUDE, I AM SO SORRY--
I KNOW. BUT WE NEED TO TALK THIS OUT.
YOU TOO, MAN.
UH, YEAH.
ME?
K.
FIRST OF ALL, AND I MEAN IT--
NEVER.
NEVER AGAIN.
WHAT HAPPENED TO YOU TODAY?
THAT'S THE THING--I'M NOT ENTIRELY SURE BUT HERE'S WHAT I KNOW...
CLICK
CLICK

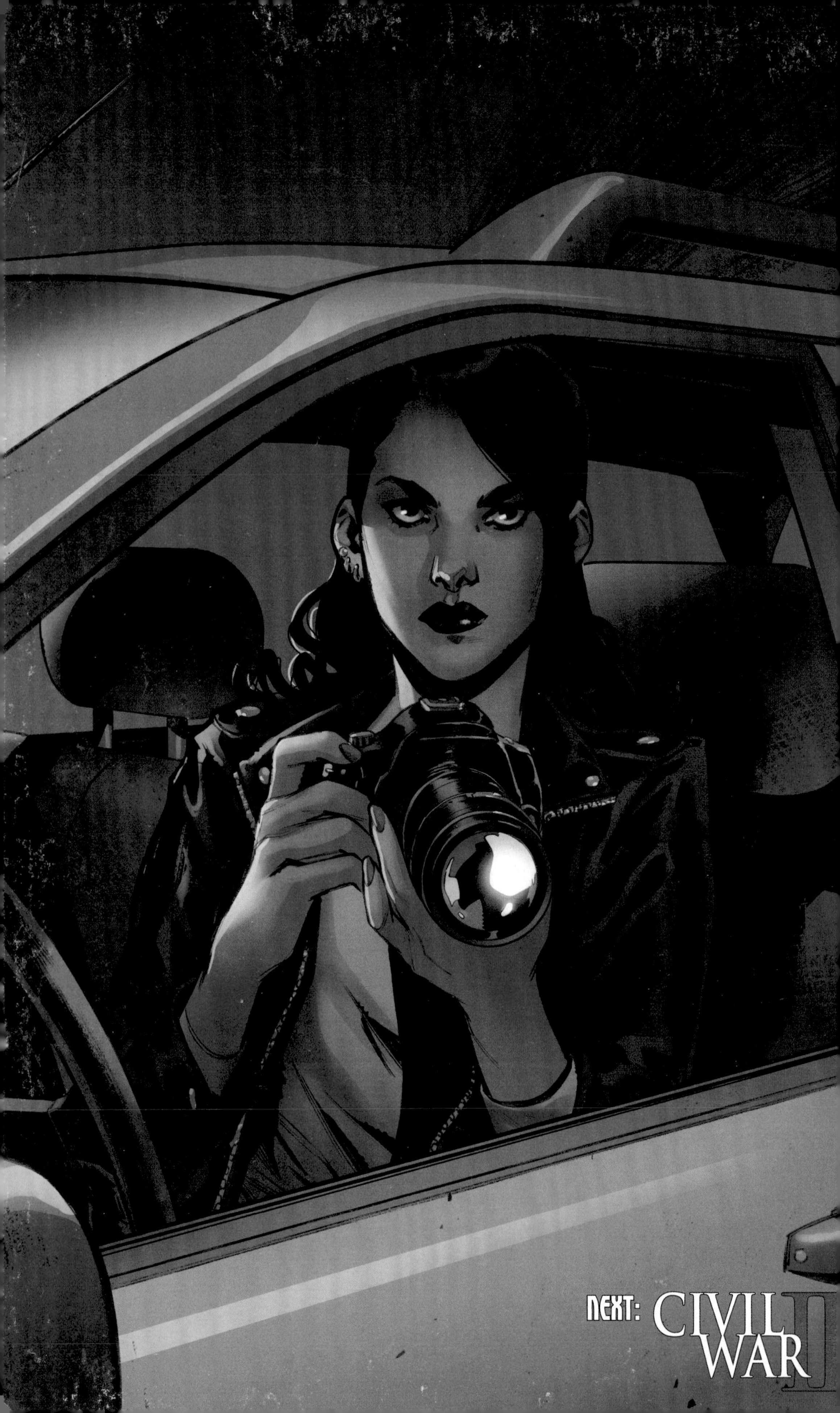
NEXT: CIVIL WAR II